NEW CENTURY READERS

The Snake-stone

Berlie Doherty

Notes: Gavin Jones

Longman

Edinburgh Gate
Harlow, Essex

Pearson Education Limited
Edinburgh Gate
Harlow
Essex
CM20 2JE
England

First published in Great Britain in 1995 by Hamish Hamilton Ltd
Copyright © Berlie Doherty 1995
The right of Berlie Doherty to be identified as the author of this
Work has been asserted by her in accordance with the Copyright,
Designs and Patents Act, 1988

This educational edition first published 2000
Editorial notes © Pearson Education Limited 2000

ISBN: 0 582 43455 6

Printed in Singapore

The Publisher's policy is to use paper manufactured from sustainable
forests

Designed and packaged by McLean Press Ltd
Cover illustration by Matthew Williams

Acknowledgement
With thanks to Sean McLevy and Simon Jackson for their advice

Contents

Introduction

About the author

I was asked to dramatise one of my teenage novels, *Dear Nobody*, for the Crucible Theatre in Sheffield, and one day in rehearsals Sean McLevy, the actor playing Chris the teenage hero, said to me 'There's a line you give me in this play that reminds me of a week in my life.'

'What's the line?' I asked, already fascinated. 'And what was the week?'

'The line is "I'm nothing to my mother now. I'm a speck of dust, and I've blown away." And the week was when I took a break from college to go in search of my mother. I'm adopted you see.'

Now he had me hooked. When I was a teenager I used to think I was adopted, and I've since found out that many teenagers have this feeling. Perhaps it's because at that age we're changing so much, but our parents aren't. They don't seem to be able to understand us any more, and surely if they were our real parents they would! We can't understand them, and we can't imagine how we can possibly have come from them. Surely our real parents must have been much more exciting! Something like that.

Anyway, I'm not adopted, nor do I have adopted children, but the idea of searching for your own history fascinated me. Everyone has a right to their own past. I knew with absolute certainty that this was what I wanted to write my next book about. I never go round searching for an idea for something to write about. That's not the way ideas come. They just happen, and there's something so true about them that somehow they won't let go, even when I'm in the middle of writing something else.

So I talked to Sean about his experience, and he told me how as a twenty-two-year-old student he'd gone to the adoption society and they'd given him all the details they'd had about his natural mother, and how he and his friend had set off 'like a couple of detectives' to the big city where his mother used to live, to see what else they could discover about her. They gave themselves a week, and as it turned out, they never actually found her.

I decided that my main character would be much younger – too young to be given this kind of information. I also decided that he would make the journey on his own, so that it would truly be a voyage of personal discovery. And though at first I thought I might make this young character a girl I decided against it, for many reasons, my main one being that I wanted to write the mother's story too. So I was writing two stories that would weave round each other, and the hero of one was fifteen-year-old James, seaching for his past, and the hero of the other was fifteen-year-old Elizabeth, who had given birth to him.

He would live in a big town, and she would be a country girl living in a Pennine valley very like my own. In this way I was getting right away from Sean's story.

I knew I was going to be writing about something very important, about belonging, and I knew also that it was a very delicate area. The last thing I wanted was for people to be hurt by my book. I thought a great deal about what it would mean to be adopted, and to give up a baby for adoption, and to adopt. All three are special situations, and I needed to put myself right inside the experience of the people. That's what being a novelist is all about. Now I was ready to set off on the journey of writing the book.

Yet, soon after starting it, I stalled.

This was a great disappointment to me, as I knew I wanted very much to write the book, yet I couldn't get moving on it. Eventually I realised that it was the central character James who was holding me back. I couldn't actually make myself believe in a boy who

2

would just head off like that without telling anyone: and if I couldn't believe in him, why should my readers? I knew I would have to develop his personality, and I decided that in order to do what he did he would have to be the sort of boy who was obsessive about things, who just wouldn't let go of something until he'd sorted it out. Musicians are like that, and sportspeople.

Sport. How about that ... the sort of boy who would kick a football into the net a hundred times a night? No, not a team sport, something very personal and individual, which would require the same sort of dedication but which would leave him on his own with his determination to succeed, and everything that came with it, the triumphs and disappointments and failures. Something dangerous perhaps, because James would be facing danger on his lonely journey. Something that requires great skill and courage, and which is also rather poetic, because James' quest is a romantic one. And then I thought of a slow-motion film I'd watched about diving, and I knew I'd found my sport.

In my valley there's a young man who used to be the European junior diving champion, and I went to talk to him. I have to confess now that nothing in the world would induce me to climb up to a ten metre board and jump off it into a little patch of water. But the more I talked to Simon Jackson the more I understood about the sheer art and precision of diving, and the way practising takes over your life. Because one false move can cost you points, or a championship, or even your life itself.

That was all I needed. I felt I knew James now, I understood him to be a boy who can drive himself to the very edge of what is bearable, and I knew I could send him off on his journey into the unknown. All this gave the story another dimension, gave me a way of linking the sort of person James is with the sort of person his mother is, bringing the past and the present together.

3

That's why the book is dedicated to Sean McLevy and Simon Jackson. It isn't their story at all, James is nothing like either of them, nor is his background at all similar to theirs, yet without Sean and Simon the book could never have been written. And in the end it isn't about a boy in search of his roots, or striving for a championship. My American publisher describes it as a kind of love story, and in a very fundamental way it is. But for James and Elizabeth it's really about facing themselves, their real selves. It's about growing up.

Berlie Doherty

Setting the scene

James Logan and his adoptive parents live in a big town. His father is a teacher and his mother works in a travel agency. James is obsessed with diving, and is continually training and practising for important competitions. Although his mother does not share James' love of diving, his father helps him enthusiastically by driving him to practice sessions and giving him extra coaching. This obsession with diving tends to isolate James from his contemporaries, and he has few real friends at school. He has always been aware that he was adopted, but has never made any attempt to find his birth (or natural) mother. One night, suddenly feeling that he doesn't belong to anybody, he starts his search. Using part of an address on a torn-off scrap of envelope on which a name has been scribbled, he sets off on a quest to find out where he came from. After a number of false starts and cases of mistaken identity, James succeeds in his quest. He meets his birth mother, and comes to some important and perhaps surprising conclusions about her, about himself and about his adoptive parents.

Main characters and summary

The two main characters in the story are James Logan and Elizabeth Frith. James is an honest person at heart and in his attempts to trace his birth mother he finds himself forced to lie to many people to hide his real intentions, as he knows that otherwise he will be prevented from continuing his search. He even risks losing his chance of working with a leading diving coach, in order to pursue his obsession – a measure of his single-mindedness and the power of the feelings which are driving him. This single-mindedness is the very quality which has up to this moment in his life made him so successful in competitive diving. During his quest, James is often surprised by the number of people he meets who are willing to help him in his search. When the trail appears to go cold, he is supported by Clair, her mother and grandmother, who encourage him to try once more. He finds a kindred spirit in Clair, who is as enthusiastic about gym as he is about his diving. At one point he even feels he might have found his sister – one of the many false trails he pursues in his search.

Elizabeth Frith is a farmer's daughter. She lives with her parents, brothers and sister in an isolated valley in the hills of Derbyshire. Elizabeth lives in a dream world in which she escapes from her harsh life in the valley. She meets a traveller boy and falls in love with him. She becomes pregnant and gives birth to a baby which she is desperate to hide for fear of her father's anger. She takes the baby over the hills to a village in another valley and leaves him outside a cottage. Some time later, she marries a local farm worker and eventually forgets all about her love affair with her 'wild boy'. The story follows the journeys made by both James and Elizabeth and their eventual meeting.

Other important characters in the story are James' adoptive parents. His mother leads a highly organised life to enable her to keep a full-time job as well as run a household. She uses machines to help reduce the housework and considers television an intruder into the house, calling it 'the uninvited guest'. While she is supportive of James' diving, she seldom attends competitions. When her daughter Rachel left home she seemed to feel that this was partly due to her husband giving undue attention to James and his diving. James describes his father rather condescendingly as 'like a big, friendly sheepdog' with whom it was impossible to be angry for long. Mr Logan takes an intense interest in James' progress in diving and perhaps at times seems to drive him too hard.

Main themes

The Snake-stone deals with a number of issues. Both the main characters feel a sense of isolation and of being different from other children of their age. They each respond in their own way to these feelings. Both feel unhappy with the lifestyles of their respective families: James with the middle-class concerns and enthusiasms of his adoptive parents and Elizabeth with her father's strictness and intolerance of other ways of life. In trying to escape from these restrictions, both James and Elizabeth break the rules of their own social groups and find themselves forced into lives of lies and deception. Elizabeth rebels against the strict social rules of the farming community where she lives, and she then believes that this is the reason for her mother's death. The wild people she refers to in her story are in fact travellers or gypsies and are regarded as wicked people by the inhabitants of the Pennine valley. Elizabeth's mother finds that her daughter is having an affair with one of the wild people. She tells her husband who takes violent action to drive the travellers away.

The author makes us think more deeply about a number of issues connected with adoption, and we see the problems connected with it from several points of view. James' adoptive parents are both very loving and supportive, but show this in different ways. James himself finds out during his adventures how much he loves and owes to his adoptive parents. He finds out what his true feelings are towards his birth mother and what her feelings seem to be towards him. We also come to understand how Elizabeth's

6

feelings about her baby alter, and what she goes through in giving him away. These issues are dealt with sensitively. The author presents us with situations and leaves us to make up our own minds about them.

Language and style

Berlie Doherty tells the story through her two main characters, James and Elizabeth. We are able to identify with each character through the language in which they speak to us – James using expressions and ideas typical of a teenage boy at an urban comprehensive school, and Elizabeth telling her story mainly in short, almost breathless and disjointed sentences. Both of them, however, break into more descriptive and colourful language when carried away by their feelings. Adult characters are presented through the eyes of the teenagers in the story – often as exasperating hindrances but also as being loving and understanding.

The story makes unusual use of time scales. As we read about James starting off on his journey of discovery and of Elizabeth struggling over the hills with her new-born baby, we only gradually discover that these events are in fact separated by 15 years. The time scale of Elizabeth's story is also not straightforward – we learn of much that has happened in a series of flashbacks. These, often dream-like sequences, parallel much of what is happening to James in his search, but whereas James' story follows a clear, unbroken sequence of time, we only gather fragments of Elizabeth's story.

As most of the story is told from the point of view of young teenagers, the author has been careful to use the sort of language we would expect of this age group. She also varies her language to portray different adults – for example, there are differences between the way Mr Griffiths, James' Humanities teacher speaks, and the language the Head uses. When we are reading Elizabeth's story, we can sense her sadness and desperation through the short, sometimes incomplete sentences she uses. She also speaks in the sort of language we might expect to find in an isolated farming community, where people may tend to be a little less talkative and to use more straightforward ways of speaking to each other. As the story develops, we can also see how both James and Elizabeth develop through the way they tell their tales. By the end of the book, James speaks with an assurance which matches his new-found confidence which comes from knowing who he is. Elizabeth, on the other hand, speaks in a relaxed, almost dreamy way which shows her acceptance of her life and her love for her husband.

The Snake-stone

Notes for Chapter 1

The first chapter is written in the first person, as if the main character (James) is actually talking to us. He captures our attention by raising a series of questions in our minds: What is so important about the stone shaped like a snake? Why does he suddenly want to find out about his past? What sort of person is he? What does he do? You also hear about other characters as James begins his story – his parents and sister (who has left home) and his trainer. You also meet the mysterious Elizabeth – but not through James' account.

What do you think?
As you read the first chapter, think about some of the following points to help you understand its structure:
- Berlie Doherty seems to be telling two stories at once. What device does she use to make it easy for us to distinguish one from the other?
- Do these two stories seem to have similar themes?
- How do you think the two stories might eventually be linked?

Questions
Look for evidence in the author's words to help you answer these questions:
1. What happens to start James on his search?
2. What are James' feelings about his parents?
3. What can we guess about Elizabeth's family and how she feels about them?
4. Do you feel sorry for James' mother when he refuses to stay and talk to her?
5. What do you think makes James say, 'I like Sammy better, that's all.'?

Further activity
Imagine that James' mother and father are discussing his behaviour and trying to decide how to react to him. Write this discussion in dramatic form, setting it out as if it were a scene from a play, with stage and set directions. Try to show your understanding of the way they live through the setting and the words they use.

Chapter 1

I have a stone that looks like a snake: all curled up. It's my most precious thing. I've had it since I was born, you see.

Do you ever think about being born?

No. I don't either. But what I do think about is this – did my mother want me?

It wasn't an easy thing to find out. I think my search all started on the night of the Big Fair.

Dad dropped me off at the park that night on his way to town. He didn't want to – in fact we had a bit of a row about it. There was a fair on in the park and because I knew most of my class were going to it I insisted on going as well. Just this once I wanted to be one of them, one of the gang, showing off to the girls. Dad just could not see the point.

'You've got the Nationals coming up next month,' he said. 'You should be doing more training, not less. I'm surprised at you, James.' He goes on and on and on, Dad does. 'I'm prepared to put in the time – why aren't you?'

It was no use trying to argue with him. I sat in the back seat and let him get on with it. Mum reached across and squeezed my hand and I knew it was going to be all right, that he'd let me go to the park, but that wasn't the point. It was the first time I had ever said that I didn't want to train, and he was acting as if it was happening all the time. He never gave me credit for the hours and hours I put in.

'I just want to be with the others, that's all,' I said. I stared out of the window, refusing to catch his eye in the driving mirror.

So he dropped me off at the park gates and drove off without saying goodbye. By this time I didn't even want to go to the fair. The other lads in the class never knocked about with me, anyway. I was never around if they wanted to. I hardly had any money on me. If I went on any of the rides I'd have to walk home. And it was raining. The grass had been churned to mud and I was wearing my new trainers. Little kids who'd lost their parents were wailing round me.

There was all kinds of screaming and shouting and laughing going on, tinny music and flashing lights. I wandered round hoping I'd see someone I knew, just so I could say 'Saw you at the fair last night' in class the next day, and then I saw Jan. Her face was damp and shining with rain and her hair stuck to her cheeks like feathers. She looked as if she was lost or lonely, the way she kept glancing round her, and I steadied myself with a deep breath and went towards her. 'Hi Jan,' I was practising, 'fancy a ride on the rollercoaster?' but before she had even noticed me her face brightened up and she went off towards a boy from another class. He had crooked teeth and he wasn't even wearing a jacket in all that rain. Her face was glowing with the different coloured lights from the rides. I'd have given anything to have been that other boy, walking along with Jan, holding her hand.

All of a sudden I didn't want to be there any more. It was the first time in my life that I'd ever felt that I didn't actually belong to anybody. That was when it began. I started thinking about my mother, and whether she had wanted me when I was born. I didn't even know her name.

They call me Elizabeth.

Sometimes I wonder whether it really happened at all. Must have done though, mustn't it — else why should I keep dreaming about it?

The belly pains came in the night. I knew what they were. I was frighted of the pains, but I knew what they were. I was frighted of screaming out loud.

When I could stand up I went outside, slow as a cow. I went to the hen-shed and lay down on the straw.

Fowls clucking and chuttering round till they went back to sleep. Just me and the pains then.

There in the dark it came slipping out. I knew what to do. I'd seen Mam having a baby, hadn't I?

Mum and Dad were still out when I got home, and I was glad. There was this beating and lurching going on in my head, this roller-coastering that was something to do with the look on Jan's face and something to do with my emptiness. It wouldn't keep quiet or still.

I went up to my room and took out the letter my diving coach in London had sent me last year. That was my most precious thing at the time.

Dear James,

I don't go in for praising much so this may be the only time I'll say it – so I thought you should have it in writing. When I watched you at the trials this last weekend I was proud of you. Very proud. I think you could go to the top, with a lot of hard work. Remember that. Every time you stand on that board I want you to say to yourself that you could be the best.

I have also seen total disasters coming from you so don't let that remark go to your head. You know who you have to beat. I personally think you can do it. Go for it!

Ken Eldred   PS Remember to STRETCH

He hadn't said a word of praise to me since, so it was worth keeping, that letter.

But reading it again that night didn't help. I still felt mixed-up and a bit lonely. I knew it was because of the way Mum and Dad had just driven away from me outside the park. It wasn't often we fell out.

I went into the room that used to be my sister's and which Dad now uses as an office. There was still a poster of Michael Jackson on the wall, from when Rachel was about twelve. I took out the box file where Dad keeps all the family papers. There was nothing secret in there, nothing I hadn't known for the whole of my life. I'd seen my papers before and I knew my story off by heart. After she'd had Rachel Mum had been told that she wouldn't be able to have another baby. She and Dad had always wanted a boy and they'd

14

chosen me. I was very special to them because they'd chosen me.

I knew all that, and yet I didn't know, if you see what I mean. I understood the words because they were familiar and easy. But it's when you start to look at words closely that they can frighten you. Every day you run downstairs without thinking about it and you arrive at the bottom safely, but the day you try to think how you actually do it you'll probably fall and break your neck. Sometimes words do that to you. There was one word in those papers that I'd known all my life and never stopped to think about, but that night, for some reason, it was blazing across the page like a fire. Adopted. That was the word.

The papers were one thing. They were there for me to look at any time I wanted to. It was what we called the baby-box that I had to look in next. I'd seen it before. It was just a box of knitted blue baby clothes and a shawl. These were the things I'd been wearing when they picked me up from the adoption society, and for some reason Mum said she couldn't bear to part with them. She keeps Rachel's baby things too, and some terrible drawings I did in my first week at school.

I was never usually interested in looking at baby clothes, of all things. But that night I was interested. I went to my parents' room and took the box out of the bottom of the wardrobe and sat on the bed with it. I picked the clothes out one by one, trying to look at them as if I'd never seen them before, the way I'd looked at that familiar word 'adopted'. They'd been laid between sheets of tissue paper with a little bag of something that made them smell sweet. Mum always puts away things like that. They looked tiny and pretty and I suppose I could tell they were well-made. I wondered whether my real mother had made them. I did something really clever then. It made me feel as if I was a super sleuth or something. I looked inside the clothes for a label to see whether they'd come from a shop. I hoped there wasn't one.

It was ridiculous, but I was really pleased to see that there wasn't. It surely meant that she had really wanted me, if she'd taken the trouble to knit baby clothes for me. They were all fancy, loopy patterns with satin ribbons threaded through, and pearly buttons. It must have taken her ages to make them. All the time she was expecting me she would have been making these clothes and thinking about me. She'd really wanted me and yet in spite of everything she'd had to give me away because she was so poor. Or maybe she'd had to leave the country in a hurry and she hadn't been able to take me with her. Maybe she was famous, a film star perhaps, and she knew she couldn't give me a proper home-life because she travelled around so much. Maybe she had died when I was born.

Mum never knits. She told me once that women who knit spend a lot of time watching television, and she certainly never does that. If she had her way we wouldn't even have a television in the house. She calls it the uninvited guest. I'm the only kid in our class who hasn't got their own television set in their bedroom.

I picked out the tiny knitted things and laid them on the bed. It made me feel strange inside, imagining myself that small, wearing tiny things like that. They weren't just clothes for a small human being, like jeans and sweat-shirts in miniature. They were soft and fluffy, as if they belonged to a little animal. I imagined my real mother dressing me in them and holding me in her arms. If anyone else had been in my room, or in the house even, I would not have looked at the baby clothes the way I did that night. It was as if I was trying to find my first self in them.

Then I heard Mum and Dad coming in. I was just about to bundle the clothes away when I saw a torn envelope in the bottom of the box. It had always been there for me to look at. Mum came into the room just as I picked it up. The handwriting was so bad that I could hardly read it. 'Look after Sammy', it said. Who on earth was Sammy?

Thought it was dead. Skinny rabbit thing gleaming in the dark. Shoved it under the straw. Crawled out to the tap in the yard and washed myself down. Dragged myself up to bed. House was breathing quiet. Little ones all asleep. Father snoring deep.

Heard screaming in my head, like the rooks in Mam's graveyard. It was so loud I thought the whole valley might wake up.

When the screaming rooks died down, heard wild horses pummelling over rocks. That was the sound of my heart inside my bones.

It was written on the back of a torn envelope that was wrapped round a stone. I was staring at something I'd seen and known all my life, but that night it wasn't clear and safe any more. It was like a muddy pool with my own face peering up from it.

Mum was surprised to see me in her room with all the baby clothes spread out over her bed. She took off her coat and yawned, as if talking was going to be a bit of an effort. Then she laughed and sat down next to me on the bed. She picked up one of the jackets.

'Just look at this, James,' she said. 'This was my favourite. Your little matineé jacket. That was what they used to call them. I suppose you were only meant to wear them in the mornings. Can you imagine fitting into that! And just look at the size of the bootees!' She put one on top of my trainer, where it sat like the flower of a foxglove or something, its satin ribbon tied in a neat bow.

'Did you knit them?' I asked. I felt a bit embarrassed about being caught drooling over baby clothes, of all things. I tried to stuff them back into the box but she stopped me.

'You know I didn't! There'd have been a few more holes in them if I had! You were wearing these the day we brought you here.'

'Did my real mother knit them?'

Mum cleared her throat slightly. 'Please call her your birth mother,' she corrected me. 'Because she gave birth to you. Or your natural mother. That's what we call her. I don't know. She might have done.' She picked up the bonnet and balanced it on top of my head. 'Just look at yourself in the mirror, James. Aren't you sweet! Little bonny blue!'

I didn't want to play. I pulled the bonnet off my head and dropped it into the box.

'Why did you call me James?' I asked her.

'It's a nice name.' She knelt down and picked up the tissue paper cloud. 'It's after your Uncle James.'

'But he isn't my uncle.'

'Of course he's your uncle.' She was folding up the tiny garments as if they were delicate flowers, as if they would crumble into pieces if she handled them roughly. 'I'm your mum, he's my brother, so he's your uncle. That's how families work.'

I watched her put away the last garment and fit the lid over it. I still had the envelope and the stone in my hand. I slid them into my pocket.

'It isn't my real name,' I said.

She swivelled round to look at me. She was smiling, but her face looked tired. She looked as if she would settle for a long talk if she had to, if that was what I really wanted. But it wasn't. I didn't really want to talk at all.

'I like Sammy better, that's all,' I said. For some reason I couldn't look at her any more. I got up and went to my own room. I slammed the door behind me. I couldn't help it.

Notes for Chapter 2

In this short chapter, we learn a little more about Elizabeth and her family. We also find out more about James and his parents. As the story develops, Berlie Doherty gives us more hints about what motivates her main characters, both through what they say and what they do.

What do you think?
As you learn more about the main characters, you may have mixed feelings about how they behave. Think about:
- how James responds to his father
- Elizabeth's feelings for the rest of her family.

Questions
Look for words and phrases in the chapter which give clues to help you answer these questions:
1. Do you feel that James is being fair to his father?
2. Why is James so keen on his swimming and diving?
3. Why do you think James suddenly remembers his red woolly horse?
4. How do James and Elizabeth react differently to the expected?
5. What do you think that James' mum is feeling in the last few paragraphs of the chapter?

Further activity
Berlie Doherty uses carefully chosen words and phrases to show James' feelings. On the left side of a sheet of paper, write down some of the words and phrases which show:
- his feelings of confusion
- his feelings of contentment or relief.

On the right side of the paper explain how you think Berlie Doherty wants you to respond to James, i.e. why she uses these particular words and phrases.

You could use a word-processor to set this out as a table. Add to your list as the story progresses.

Chapter 2

I lay awake thinking, what if Caroline finds it? What if Father finds it? Thought of little Michael rummaging in the straw for the eggs, finding skinny dead rabbity thing.

Put my clothes on. Couldn't stop shaking, couldn't stop sobbing. Wanted Mam. Put the coat on that Father bought me for Mam's funeral, and then my boots from the porch.

Got the spade.

Went out to the hen-barn. Scared to go in.

Dad woke me up at six next morning. By the time I'd struggled out of my coma and found my way into the clean tracksuit Mum had put out for me he was already in the car, revving up the engine. I swallowed some milk and slid into the car next to him, checking my sandwiches, my school things, my sportsbag with the swimming gear. It was still raining. We drove along in silence until we got into town.

'Your mother was upset last night,' Dad said. 'Is there anything you want to know about being adopted?' He looked round at me. 'Always ask, won't you? We'll tell you as much as we know.'

'It's all right,' I said. I stared out of the side window. 'I just didn't know I used to be called Sammy.'

Dad pulled into the car-park opposite the Leisure Centre.

'Well, it was always there for you to see. We've never hidden anything from you.'

'I know. I know,' I muttered. I couldn't explain to him how muddled up I felt, or how hard it was to talk about it. I didn't even want to talk about it then. I zipped up my jacket and leaned back over the seat to reach for my sportsbag. Dad got out of the car and stood waiting for me.

'You were very young when you were taken to the adoption society. You'd hardly had time to be called anything. Sammy was just like a label.'

I slammed my door. I didn't mean to.

'We wanted to give you a name of our own, a name we'd chosen ourselves. We both liked the name James very much. It suited you. It still does.'

I kept thinking about the little blue jacket with the shiny ribbons. That suited me once.

'Sammy was a strange name to us. A stranger's name.' Dad does go on. I think it's because he's a teacher. He has to make sure in his head that you understand exactly what he's saying. It can be very boring. Sometimes it can really hurt, because he won't let go, even when you're upset. Surely he can see when you're upset. 'We'd already thought of James, when we were waiting for the adoption society to find the right boy for us. Most parents do that. Choosing a name is a way of making the child real.'

I felt helpless. Dad put his arm across my shoulder. I looked round, hoping that none of the others from the diving club had arrived.

'I'll be late, Dad,' I said. He laughed as I tried to squirm away.

'A dad can hug his lad, can't he? Off you go then, no point in us both getting wet. See you tonight, James.'

I sprinted over the road. I didn't feel confused any more. I felt great. Dad was like a big, friendly sheepdog at times. You couldn't be upset with him for long.

I love being the first one in the pool. It's as smooth as glass. Nothing is so still and so quiet. When you look down into it it's so clear you feel sure that there's no water in it at all. It's like breaking a spell, diving head down into it, shattering it. I wish I could always be the first to break it. But that morning the police were there already, doing their fitness training. I just plunged in and ploughed up and down the lane, twenty, thirty, forty lengths, head up every now and then to look at the clock, because I had to be on the bus for school at eight. All of a sudden a thought bobbed its way into my brain as if it was a goldfish that had come bubbling its way through the swimming pool. The envelope was still in my jeans pocket. What if Mum put them in the washing machine! I've never felt so close to panic as I did then, scrambling out of the pool. It was then that I realised that the Sammy note and that little twisted stone meant more to me than any of my diving trophies.

Shushed to the hens; 'Shush-shush, come cluckety-cluck,' like I always do.

Went to the straw pile and knelt down.

Felt for the skinny dead thing. It moved in my hand.

23

Could have dropped it. Could have screamed out loud. Wanted Mam.

I knew what to do with a dead baby.

Dig a deep hole and bury it there.

I didn't know what to do with a live one.

I towelled myself down without going under the shower, then ran to the phone in the foyer. It wasn't working. I could have pulled it out of the wall, I was so pent-up and frustrated. Mum always put the washing on before she went out to work at the travel agency. She calls the washing-machine and the dishwasher her servants because they just get on with the jobs, bubbling away in the empty house while she's out doing more interesting things. The Sammy note would be reduced to pulp. I felt as if I had lost my only contact with my real self.

While I was standing there dithering and shivering I kept thinking about a little red woolly horse with long ears that I used to have when I was about three. I used to take it everywhere, dragging it along by its tail, and one day a dog had a go at it and started mauling it to death. Mum managed to rescue it but it was reduced to tatters, its insides dripping yellow sponge and one of its ears pulled off, and it was all slimy from being in the dog's mouth.

I raced to the bus depot and just managed to catch a bus as it was pulling out. My ears were full of swimming pool and there was a cold stream running down the back of my neck. It took forever to get through town because of all the roadworks and diversions but at last we were at the roundabout at the bottom of my road. I sprinted up the hill and just arrived as Mum was closing the front door.

'James! What's happened?'

I could hardly speak for panting. You'd think I'd be fit, all the swimming and diving I do. 'My jeans!' I managed to croak out. 'Have you washed them?'

'Of course I have. I've just switched on the servants.'

I pushed past her into the kitchen, and stood in despair watching the slow swirl of blue clothes. I tried to wrench open the door.

'What on earth do you think you're doing?' Mum shouted. 'We'll have water all over the kitchen floor.'

'But I left something in my pocket ...'

Mum picked up her bag and went back to the front door. 'Try looking on your bed, James.'

She went out quickly to catch her bus and I ran up the stairs two at a time. There on the bed, among the jumble of elastic bands, comb, coins, half-eaten Mars bar and the concertina I'd been making out of bus tickets, were the Sammy note and the little stone.

I remembered then, too late, that I'd left my sportsbag with all my schoolwork inside it at the Leisure Centre.

Notes for Chapters 3 and 4

The differences between Elizabeth's fear of her father and James' desire to please his parents are brought out more clearly at the start of Chapter 3. There is more about James' trainer and Matt, who shares the coaching sessions. The close relationship between James and his parents, restored in the early part of Chapter 3, is destroyed again by an accident. In Chapter 4 James feels resentment as his father forces him to dive once more.

What do you think?
In these two chapters, Berlie Doherty makes much of the dedication needed to become an expert in any activity. She shows how such dedication can cause tensions and lead to violent reactions when things go wrong. As you read these chapters, think about:
- James' explanation of why his training meant so much to him
- his desire to confide in someone other than his adoptive parents
- why there is no reference to Elizabeth in Chapter 4.

Questions
Think about how the author presents the events in these chapters to help you answer the following questions:
1. How does James try to make it up to his parents?
2. Why do you think Rachel's leaving home made James determined never to let his father down?
3. Do you think that James' father is right to make him dive again?
4. James twice uses the fact of his adoption to hurt his parents. Is he justified? Do you think he really understands how they feel about him?

Further activity
James prepares a meal as a sort of peace offering for his parents. Other ways in which he might have expressed his feelings could include:
- a letter (not necessarily to his parents – who else might he write to?)
- an entry in his diary.

Choose one of the above and write it as if you were James. You will need to show that you understand his way of thinking and the language he is likely to use.

Chapter 3

Hide it, hide it from Father. That was the only thing in my mind then. Found a sack and wrapped it round like a sick lamb. Ran out in yard with it tucked inside my coat. Had to take it somewhere before Father got up.

Lonely. So much dark around.

Heard Bob whimpering. Let him out. Come with me, Bob. I was frighted on my own. He licked my hand, licked my face as I bent down to him.

My belly hurt so bad. Ached and ached with all that kicking inside it when the thing came out.

Where can I go, Bob, where I won't be seen?

Where can I go so no one tells on me to Father?

I was put in detention that night for being late for registration. It didn't really matter. It was the Griffin in charge and he let me do my homework instead of the mindless lists that some of the teachers give you to do in detention. *I must not be late for school* three hundred times in your best handwriting. What a waste of trees. When I'd finished my homework I wrote up my diving log.

What is my short-term aim? To do a two-and-a-half times reverse somersault. Also to get in the water without splashing. What is my long-term aim? To get to the top. Exercises done this week. Every night except Wednesday; 30 press-ups, 10 armstand press-ups, 40 sit-ups. Health: a bit of a cold.

I was still home before Mum and Dad. I decided to make them a curry for a treat. I always make a curry when

I have a chance. It's really easy. You just chop up an onion and some garlic and let them fry a bit and you add what Mum calls the three C spices, cumin, coriander and cardamon, only sometimes I just chuck in a load of mixed curry powder. Then you throw in anything you can find that's left over in the fridge and you add a tin of tomatoes and a bit of lemon juice. I can't do rice, though. It always either sogs up like a pudding or it stays as hard as grit and breaks your fillings.

All the time I was doing the chopping and stirring and tasting I was thinking about Mum and Dad. I suppose I wanted to make it up to them for the way I'd behaved. I knew I must have hurt them, especially Dad. I thought of the way he takes me down the Leisure Centre for swimming every morning, and for diving and ground-work coaching three times a week. He didn't have to do it. It wasn't his fault that I was mad on diving. He even paid for me to go to London sometimes for special coaching with Ken Eldred. He never grumbled about it. He came to all the competition meets. He even went on a coaching course so he could give me extra coaching when Whisky Mac wasn't around. If anything, he was keener than I was. I did it all for love, because I was crazy about diving, because I couldn't think about anything else.

Every nerve in my body and every thought in my mind was keyed up to it. I dreamed dives.

Dad got it into his head that I'd be county champion, then British Junior champion. He wanted me to dive for England in Internationals. That was all his idea. He was proud of me. Mum never came to the meets. She polished my trophies, though. She was just as proud of me, in her own way.

I heard her arguing with Dad about it once. It was the day my sister Rachel had told us that she was leaving home. She wanted to move into a flat with her best friend. Mum had sat in a sort of white, drained silence while Rachel was telling us this, and when Rachel had gone out she had turned to Dad and shouted at him,

'See what you've done, with all this diving!'

I hadn't a clue what she was talking about. It wasn't Dad who was diving, it was me. But when Rachel had left and there was no more loud music blasting from her room, no cascade of underclothes dripping over the bath, no mess of eyeliner and hair mousse in the sink, I think I knew what she meant.

Whatever happened, I wouldn't let Dad down.

So I made a steamy curry and waited for them to come home. While I was waiting I went up to my room and had a proper look at the stone in my Sammy note envelope. It was an odd thing, a bit like a snail shell, curled up on itself in a spiral. I liked the feel of it in my hand, because it was worn smooth and polished. I wondered if my real mother had bought it specially for me, or found it somewhere. It seemed a funny thing to want to give a new-born baby. It must have some kind of special meaning, like a lucky charm.

The curry smelt fantastic. I got tired of waiting for Mum and Dad so I ate some. It was so good that I ate some more, and while I was eating it they arrived home, cold and tired and pleased to smell the food. Mum peered into the pan.

'You might have left a bit more,' she said. She scooped out the remains on to a plate and handed it to Dad. 'Pity. I love your curry.'

I was really disappointed. I would have perked it up with another tin of tomatoes or something if she'd given me time.

'There's plenty of rice left,' I said.

'You have it,' Dad told her. 'It's nearly time to take James for his coaching. I'll have a sandwich in the car.'

'I'll go on the bus,' I volunteered. I actually felt too full to dive, but I didn't dare tell him that. I could have done with a walk first.

'No, you don't,' said Dad. 'It's Thursday. I'm coaching you and Matt tonight, remember.'

I really used to like Thursday nights. My usual coach was Whisky Mac, who was shaped like a balloon and couldn't bend to pick up a flyer, let alone demonstrate a tuck, though he was a brilliant coach. But on Thursdays Matt came over on the train and he and I had the evening together, with Dad supervising. It was a good laugh. I suppose Matt was my only real friend, which was a bit odd because he was also my greatest rival. He lived about thirty miles away so we only ever saw each other at competitions, and sometimes at Ken Eldred's club in London. I was really pleased when Dad suggested giving us a bit of extra coaching together. Matt was made like an elastic band. I've never seen anyone so flexible. He could do anything except make a clean entry into the water. I could do anything in the air but my take-offs were dodgy. Between us we'd have made a pretty good diver, we reckoned. If Matt learnt a new dive before I did the only thing I could think of was catching up and doing it better than he did, and he was the same with me. Reverse two-and-a-half somersault, that was the dive we both hankered after at the moment. It would take weeks of groundwork before we were ready to do it off the board.

So on Thursdays Dad would pick Matt up from the station and take us both down and just concentrate on take-offs and entries. He never coached us in any of the fancy dives, and he never commented on style or anything. That was Whisky Mac's job. But Dad would get us doing our basic pikes a million times over. You'd think we'd get sick of it but we didn't. It was a drug – get it right, get it right, get it right. And when you did get it right you did it again, and again, and again. I've heard kids in the music room at school playing the same scales over and over till I could go down and murder them, but at least I understood why they did it. Every time is a fresh start, a new challenge. Net practice, sprint starts, it's all the same. Whisky Mac's motto is, 'The fancy stuff is sheer inspiration but the basics are what make you perfect.' The only thing is, you're never perfect. Not with Dad for a coach.

Matt and I were really tired after nearly three hours of just doing the same straight dive to get clean take-offs and entries. We'd got to the stage of nearly hating Dad, we were so exhausted. He never praised and never wanted to give up. They're all the same, all the coaches I've ever met. They might be really nice guys out of the pool but they turn into pyschos inside them. They have to be like that, I suppose. You'd never be able to force yourself to train that way, right up to the limits. But no one should push you beyond the limits, the way Dad did that night.

'That's enough springboard practice,' he shouted at last, and we loped along out of the pool. I kicked over on to my back because I was too tired to swim out. As I reached for my towel Dad pulled it out of the way.

'I want one from the ten-metre board before we go,' he said.

'Dad!' I moaned.

'Do it!'

It's a long way up to the top high board. I never really liked it as much as the springboard. You're ten metres from the water and fifteen metres from the bottom of the pool. That's twice the height of our house. But you don't look down. If you lose your nerve you feel as if you're on a cliff edge somewhere half-way up a mountain. Everything about the takeoff is different, because you're just standing on a block of concrete. It's more like gymnastics, only the floor is that deep concrete base of the pool, miles below the blue.

Matt went off first with a perfect back somersault,

grinning widely at me as he went. I just did a pike. I really was too tired to do any showing off. My entry was classic, without a hint of splash. Matt yodelled with triumph from the side. Dad should have been satisfied.

'One more for luck.'

Matt sank down on to his knees and pretended to be praying, but Dad didn't even smile.

'One more, and we'll stop for a beefburger on the way home. And chips.'

We hauled ourselves up the steps, Matt first.

'What does the guy want?' he asked me.

'A two-and-a-half reverse summy standing on a monocycle,' I suggested.

'I forgot to bring the bike,' Matt said. 'Do you think he'll notice?'

I laughed and gave him the thumbs up from my end of the board.

He positioned himself as if he was really going to do it, pretending to pedal a bike up and down the board, measuring the board, pretended to lose his nerve and topple off the bike. We both watched it splash into the water. We were in hysterics. I think that was because we were both so tired.

'Get on with it!' Dad bellowed.

Matt pulled a face, turned, ran to the end, paused for only a second, turned again to jump, and as he flipped over, the top of his head cracked against the board. I'll never forget the sound of that crack, ever.

Chapter 4

With that sickening crack still chiming in my head I slithered somehow down all the steps and raced over to where Dad and Darren the attendant were hauling Matt out the water. He looked dead to me. Darren gave him mouth to mouth resuscitation and at last Matt gulped a bit and started coughing up water, but he didn't open his eyes and he didn't move. We covered him with dry towels and blankets. There was no colour in his face at all. And do you know what Dad said to me as we were crouched over Matt, waiting for the ambulance?

'You haven't done your dive yet,' he said.

'Dad …?'

'Go on. Do it.'

'I can't. Not now.'

'Do it James.'

He put his hand out towards me and I flinched away. I couldn't believe what he was asking me to do.

'If you don't do it now, you'll never want to go up on that high board again.'

I really hated him. I hauled myself up those steps as if I was going to the gallows. I could feel my life draining away from me. I could hardly lift my legs, they were like blocks of concrete. When I got to the top board I thought I was going to vomit. I walked to the end and the air started swinging round me in a baffle of white lights and sparkle and blue water drops. I knew then what fear is all about. It clenches at your guts and turns your limbs into liquid. It shreds you into pieces.

I didn't dare look down. I stood at the edge of the board and my arms swung automatically into position. I was saying inside myself, 'If there is a God, help me, help me, help me.' And then I heard myself shouting, or a voice a bit like mine, but cracked up and ragged:

'You've no right to do this to me. You're not even my father.'

When I came up out of the water he wasn't even watching.

The ambulance arrived before I was dressed. Darren went with Matt to the hospital and Dad followed in his car. He wouldn't let me go with him. He gave me the money for a taxi home but I didn't use it. Instead I walked, all three and a half miles. I was dog-tired and cold, and the curry I'd eaten seemed to belong to another day. I just needed to make sense of something that was spinning round and round in my head, the way a moth flutters round your room at night and won't let you sleep. I kept imagining telling all this to my mother, my real mother, the one who had given birth to me and who had had to give me away. I wanted to know what she would have thought if she had known about all this. I had an aching in me that I'd never felt before. I wanted to know what she was like.

By the time I arrived home Dad was already back from the hospital. He and Mum were both worried and upset, standing in the kitchen as if they didn't know what to do with themselves. I went straight to my room and Dad followed me up. He was the last person I wanted to talk to. He sat on the edge of my bed and I stood with my back to him, willing him to go away.

'Matt's parents are with him now.'

'Oh,' I said. 'He's not dead then.' It sounded callous, the way I blurted it out, but I couldn't think of any other way to say it. It was the only thing I wanted to know.

'No. He was still unconscious.'

'So he might die?'

'I don't know, James. I just don't know. The doctors will talk to his parents. I'm sure he'll be all right.'

'You shouldn't have made him do it.' My throat was so clenched up that I could hardly get the words out. Someone had to be blamed. A boy like Matt couldn't just die, just like that.

'Maybe I shouldn't. Maybe he shouldn't have been messing about like that.'

'And then you go and make me dive, after all that. Did you want to kill me, too?'

I was aware of Mum standing in the doorway with a tray of hot drinks. I could see her sad, shocked face, and Dad twisting away from me; big, laughing, noisy Dad without a word to say to defend himself. I wanted to hurt him as much as he'd hurt me.

Mum set the tray down and tried to put her arms round me. I twisted away. I wanted to hurt her, too.

'You're upset, James,' she said. 'We're all upset. It was a

terrible thing. All we can do now is wait for news from Matt's parents.'

'I'll phone the hospital again.' Dad's voice was husky. As he went out Mum gave me one of the hot drinks.

'Your father made you do that last dive for your sake, not his. Do you think it was easy for him? How on earth do you think he felt about risking his own son after what had happened to Matt?'

I felt as if I was a million miles away from her. She searched my eyes for an answer. I couldn't give her the one she wanted.

'I'm not, though,' I said. 'I'm not his son.'

Notes for Chapter 5

James has the chance to go to London for a week's coaching while his parents are away. He starts to plan how he could trace his natural mother. We also pick up Elizabeth's story again and follow her journey.

What do you think?

Think about:

- how James' parents show concern for his feelings and work hard to avoid arguing with him
- the difference between the way James' parents speak and the language Elizabeth uses
- how the theme of journeying is important to the story.

Questions

Look closely at the language used to help you answer these questions:

1. Is there enough information on the torn envelope for James to find out the full address? How might he go about this?

2. How is Elizabeth's fear of the mountain shown?

3. How has his father's behaviour changed on the morning after the accident? Why do you think this might be?

4. What does James mean when he says his parents 'must have been practising all night'?

5. On page 44 James pictures himself as a fish. How does the language create this impression?

Further activity

Choose someone to interview who has a particular interest or who is an expert in some activity. Prepare a list of questions. Record your interview or make brief notes as you go. Then write up your interview, for example, as an item for a school newsletter. What conclusions do you reach about people who have such interests?

Don't forget to: check that the person is willing to be interviewed; make sure your teacher or parents know what you are doing; offer to report your findings back to the person you have interviewed.

Chapter 5

I couldn't sleep that night. Whenever I closed my eyes I saw Matt plunging like a shot bird out of the sky. I hadn't seen his fall, of course, I'd been above it, but I'd heard the crack of his head and the kind of yelp Dad and Darren had given, the broken splash as he crashed through the surface of the pool.

During the night I got up and started looking for my Sammy note. I couldn't remember where I'd left it. When I found it, tucked inside one of my trophies, I sat holding it and looking at it and gradually hearing a clear voice in my head. It was as if I had found someone to talk to. I think my mother would have known what to say to me about Matt.

I turned the note over and looked at the strange scribbled words on the other side. I realised for the first time that what I was reading was the remains of an address, ripped across slantways. I was only seeing the right-hand corner of it. The first letter could have been 'm' or it could have been 'on', it was almost impossible to tell:

I knew with a slow, rich kind of longing that this must be where my mother lived. If I wanted to I could find her.

Had to take it right away from home.

Someone would see me if I went to the village or down the lane to the main road. Someone would see me and tell Father. He would kill me if he knew.

I turned my back against the house, where the little ones were sleeping warm in their beds and Father was snoring.

I knew I had to take the skinny thing over the mountain tor.

Big, massy shape in the dark.

Never been up there, right to the top and over to the other side.

They say planes crashed up there in the war, and the pilots were never found, and it's haunted by them.

They say boggarts climb out of the peat to lure you into the marshes.

The wind was full of sleet and squall. The little thing started to whimper, like a cat.

Pulled my coat tight round it. Went past Uncle Staff's lambing sheds with Bob scampering round my knees. No one about. Too early yet. Too early for the birds to start shouting.

I was too sore to climb over the stile. Had to put bundle down in mud while I opened the gate.

Bob snuffled his face into it and I yanked him back.

Picked it up and shoved it back inside my coat. Felt it moving itself around.

Wondered if it would die before I got over the tor.

Wanted to find somewhere safe for it.

Didn't want it to die.

Dad came up to my room the next morning at the usual time. I was awake anyway. Usually, however warm the bed was, I'd be up like a shot when he woke me because the old adrenalin would be pumping through my veins and yelling at me to get up and get on with my diving. But I didn't want to go back to the pool that day or ever again. Not with him.

Dad opened my door but didn't come into my room.

'Matt's been moved to his local hospital,' he told me. 'I think that's a good sign, James. And Mum's going to drop you off at the pool. She wants to get to work early.'

I said nothing. At least I wouldn't have to go with him. Mum hardly ever took me to the pool, and she certainly wouldn't want to come inside. She hated the smell of chlorine. It made her feel sick, she said. And it was too echoey for her liking. I loved everything about it, usually.

'I don't think I'll go today,' I said.

Dad stood at the door, looking away from me down the landing. I wondered whether Mum was standing there watching him.

'I've been thinking, James,' he said at last. 'I don't feel I should try to coach you any more.'

I lay quite still, staring up at the ceiling. A web was hanging from it, swirling slightly in the draught from the door.

'It's not such a good idea. We'll only fall out, and I don't want that. And I don't think I know enough.'

If he wanted consolation from me he wasn't going to get

any. He stood for a bit with his hand on the door knob. I didn't even hear him go.

I slid out of bed and dressed in my school clothes, found a towel and wrapped up my trunks. When I went downstairs Dad had gone to his school on the bus and Mum was waiting for me with the car keys in her hand. I wish they didn't make it so easy for me. I wanted to dive for myself, for fun. They were trying to turn it into a duty. They didn't understand. It had nothing to do with them.

As soon as we got into the car Mum picked up the conversation where Dad had left off. They must have been practising all night.

'We thought we'd arrange for you to have a week's special coaching in London at half-term,' she said. 'Ken Eldred would be pleased to have you, I'm sure, and then you can go to him every weekend if that works out.'

Ken was my coach at Crystal Palace. He was a superb coach. Normally I'd have been over the moon with the suggestion.

'Why?' I asked.

'It's your last chance to win the Junior National title. You'd have a week of real intensive coaching. Do it for your dad,' she said, glancing at me quickly as we pulled up at traffic lights. 'He'd love you to win that. It means so much to him. And to me. You might be winning the Olympics one day!' She stalled the car as she said that, and I looked away. She'd never been on a diving board in

42

her life. She couldn't even swim. She hadn't a clue what she was talking about.

'I hate it when you say that,' I said. I suppose it came out a bit loud.

'We're all under a bit of a strain,' she said. 'Aren't we?'

I nodded, trying to clear my throat.

'And a week away from each other won't do us any harm.'

'No. I don't suppose it would.'

Mum loves to organise people. I suppose that's because of her job. People who come to her want her to arrange their holidays and travel timetables for them. I don't think she realises how annoying it is when she does it for everyone else, too.

'I'm going to take your dad up to Scotland for a few days. Uncle James invited us to spend half-term with him, and of course Dad wouldn't hear of it at first because of your training. But I …' she pursed her lips and then sighed. 'I'm sorry, but I would actually like a holiday miles away from a swimming pool.'

'Of course.'

'Have a think about it, James.'

I wondered then if Mum resented the time Dad spent with me as much as Rachel had done. He was with me every morning first thing, most evenings at the pool or the gym, and sometimes he even drove down to London with me and stayed over. He came to every single meet with me. I'd never thought of that before.

As we drew up opposite the Leisure Centre I noticed

her AA road atlas on the car shelf. I picked it up and leafed through it. 'Don't need this today, do you?'

She was surprised. I think she was waiting for a response to everything she'd been saying, but as far as I could tell the only option was to agree with her.

'I should think I can get to work without it. Why?'

'I need it for my humanities project.' I stuffed it in my bag as I was getting out. The lights changed and Mum pulled away quickly, lifting up her hand in a wave of goodbye, and with a surge of remembered dread I realised that neither of us had mentioned Matt. It was as if all the horror of last night had just been part of a dream. I walked across the road into the Leisure Centre as if I was floating back into a nightmare. None of the attendants at the pool knew anything about it, didn't know Matt because he only came on a Thursday night, didn't even know Darren.

The early morning sun was coming through the high windows on to the pool, dappling it to gold. I plunged in from the side and let my feet propel me along, feeling the silky watery air around me buoying me up, twisting and turning over and over in it. I was a fish, and this was my element. I curled myself up, clasping my knees, rotating slowly under the water. I thought of my curled-up stone. I untwisted and piked up, fish again.

I heard a shout and surfaced, bewildered. I'd forgotten where I was. A hunky swimmer with shoulders like a wardrobe and black rubber-goggled eyes ploughed towards me. He twisted his head round and jetted a plume of water out of the corner of his mouth. 'Stick in your lane, sonny,' he crooned, 'unless you want a noseful of elbow, right?'

Right.

Stopped for a rest when I came to the bridge.

Wanted to sleep there. Wanted to sleep and sleep for ever. Wanted to forget all that pain.

Inside my coat it started to cry again.

Wanted to shake the crying out of it. Held it out over the water. 'Could drop you in,' I said. 'Could drop you in and then you wouldn't cry no more.'

Thought of last summer, when I came here with the wild boy. Thought how we swam and laughed in that water down below the bridge.

Remembered showing him how I could twist in the air before I touched the water.

Water bird. That's what the wild boy called me.

Notes for Chapter 6

The author tells us more about James' school, introducing some of his fellow pupils and teachers. He is encouraged in his diving by the Head. Elizabeth continues her journey, remembering how her mother would have encouraged her. James learns more about his snake-stone from Mr Griffin, his Humanities teacher. He enlists Mr Griffin's help in finding the place mentioned on the torn slip of envelope.

What do you think?

In this chapter you will notice that James' teachers are interested in him and what he is doing. You will also have seen that not all his fellow pupils are friendly towards him. As you read, think about:

- the different ways in which the teachers and pupils react to James
- how single-minded James is about the things that interest him.

Questions

Look for evidence in how the characters behave and speak to James to help you answer these questions:

1. What impression does James give us of the Head's attitude to her job?
2. What sort of relationship does James have with the teachers we meet in this chapter?
3. What does the author want you to think about James' feelings about his school?
4. What do we learn about James when he is confronted by Pieface Mygrove and Digger?
5. How does the author manage to keep our attention towards the end of the chapter?

Further activity

Many people experience bullying of one kind or another at some time in their lives. How might you advise a newcomer to your school to cope with possible bullying? Prepare a leaflet setting out your advice in an easy-to-read format. This could be done using a word-processor and including eye-catching illustrations and presentational devices, such as frames, headings, etc., where appropriate.

Chapter 6

During Humanities that afternoon I was called to see the Head. We had been put into groups of four to work on a project and I was the odd one out. I didn't mind. I could have squeezed in with any of the groups if I'd made a fuss but I actually preferred to work on my own. I just can't concentrate with people jabbering round me. If I could get my work over and done with at school it would give me more of the evening free. There were only two groups I would have wanted to be in, anyway. One was Digger's. He used to be my friend, right through Junior school, until I started having intensive coaching and he found better things to do than to hang round waiting for me. I didn't really know how to talk to him any more. He had a way of looking at me sometimes and grinning that made me wonder whether he was laughing at me. All the same, it would have been fun to be in his group.

He goes round with Lestor Mygrove now. I call him Pieface. His face is round and white like uncooked pastry, and his eyes are like the slits Mum cuts for the gravy to ooze through. The worst thing is, he was trying to grow a beard once but he had no chance. Even before the Head made him shave it off he was on to a loser if he expected cred. from it. All it amounted to were a few wispy tufts on his chin as if someone had dropped his pieface on the floor and it still had bits of carpet fluff stuck to it. The other bad thing was that he was as tall as anyone else in the school and he threw himself around as if the world belonged to him. The worst thing of all was that Digger seemed to like him.

The other group, of course, was Jan's, but they were all girls together at that table, all giggling a bit about something. I wondered whether Jan knew that I was watching her, and whether she really liked the boy with the teeth. When she looked up I glanced out of the window, conscious of my neck going red.

So I was quite relieved when someone came with a message for me to go to the Headteacher's office. I felt self-conscious walking down the room, though.

'Been winning another competition, James?' Mr Griffiths asked.

'Not that I know of, Sir,' I said, and someone from Jan's table giggled. If anyone else had been called to the Head we would have assumed it meant trouble, so I should have been grateful, but I wasn't. I was embarrassed. Digger tried to trip me up when I went past his desk, but when I looked round at him he gave me his usual cheery grin. I don't know whether he likes me or not, really.

The Head has a big study overlooking the school playing fields. Her door was open, and I could see her standing by the window watching a dog.

'You wanted to see me,' I said to her back. 'James Logan.'

'Ah,' she said. 'Our diver. Just a minute, James. I need to speak to the caretaker.'

She went past me down the corridor, the green laces on her shoes tapping rapidly on the floor. I wondered whether she was anything like my real mother. This thought had never struck me before. I usually think of my mother as being someone young and pretty, like Digger's mother, who comes to parents' evenings in a shimmer of long silvery hair and dazzling ear-rings.

Soon I saw the Head and the caretaker out on the field and I went to watch the fun out of the window. The caretaker was chasing the black and white dog, who seemed to think it was all a wonderful game, and the Head was bending down with a little pan and brush picking up the deposits it had left. That's one thing about our Head. Her favourite assembly motto was 'Never ask someone to do something you wouldn't do yourself.' It was good to know she actually meant it. All the same, I ducked down when she came past the window holding the shovel well in front of her. It was not the most dignified thing in the world for a headteacher to be doing.

The fact was, though, that she had wasted ten minutes of the lesson by doing it. I wondered whether I should say 'It's all right, it doesn't matter' when she apologised about it, or whether that would be giving her the impression that I didn't like Humanities. As it happened she didn't apologise at all. She came in rubbing her hands together and with her cheeks as red as tomatoes. I really think she'd been enjoying herself out there.

'Ah, James! Your father rang,' she said, suddenly serious. 'It was about your friend Matthew.'

'He's not really my friend. I didn't know him very well.'
I suppose I wanted to make things easier for her. I didn't
want to hear what she had to tell me. I wanted her eager,
tomatoey face to look away from me so I didn't have to
show her how I felt. I stared beyond her at the playing
fields, where the black and white dog was hurling himself
at the caretaker.

'It's all right, James. He's regained consciousness. Still
very poorly, but off the danger list. I thought it was very
good of your father to phone up. You must have been very
worried.'

I tried to swallow, and couldn't.

'It'll be all right now, you'll see. I suppose it was a
diving accident?'

'It wasn't Matt's fault. It was my dad's.' I kept my eyes
on the dog, and my hands bunched up in my pockets.

'Then think how dreadful your father must be feeling.'

She has a nice voice, the Head. Even when she's talking
to us all in assembly she never shouts. It's not shrill, like
some women's voices. And when she said that about Dad
she was speaking very softly, so the words got right inside
my head. I wondered whether my mother had a soft, kind
voice like that.

'I ran over a cat once,' she went on. 'It wasn't my fault.
It just ran out in front of my car. I couldn't do anything to
avoid it. I can hear it now, the thud of its little body
against the wheel. I'll always feel guilty.'

She turned away from me towards the window and
sighed. 'Run round the field on your way back to class

and get that dog off the pitch for me. It'll do you good and save Mr Robinson's legs. I think the dog's actually playing with him.'

That would just about finish off my Humanities lesson for me. I wondered whether she cared about my future at all.

'What's coming up next for you?' she asked, as if she was reading my thoughts. 'European Championships?'

'That's in the summer holidays,' I said. 'After the Nationals. There's a meet next weekend, but that's just local.'

'Good,' she said. The phone rang and she picked it up instantly, cupping her hand over the mouthpiece. 'Olympics next, James.'

It did feel good to be jogging round the field with that crazy dog prancing round me. Matt was getting better. With or without him in the running I was still the favourite for the British Championships. That meant I was on target for Europe. And as for the Olympics – somebody had to be there in the British squad. Why not me?

I couldn't do it. It was too hard and too high. Dark and cold on the mountain-side. Rain like little stones on my face.

My belly pained me and my legs were tottering.

But the baby thing was crying inside my coat.

Couldn't leave it there. Had to force myself to go up.

Had to say, 'Elizabeth, Elizabeth, you do it, girl.' That's what Mam would have said to me.

When I was back in class I got out Mum's road atlas book and started flicking through it. There was no point even pretending to catch up with the lesson. I'd left the Sammy note at home in the trophy but I'd copied out the letters into my notebook. I opened it at the right page and put the swirly stone next to it, like a kind of charm.

Mr Griffiths came and stood behind me, looking over my shoulder. I knew he wouldn't mind. It's anything for a quiet life with the Griffin. So long as no one's actually disrupting the class he doesn't really mind what you do. He comes to school on his push-bike and wheels it down the corridor to the staff-room in case it gets nicked from the bike-sheds. Nothing's safe in our school. We carry everything round with us; sports gear, coats, instruments if we're doing music. Everyone lumbers round school like a crowd of refugees carting all their worldly possessions with them. Put anything down and it's gone for ever. So when the Griffin reached over me to pick up my stone my hand streaked out instinctively to cover it up.

'Can I have a look at your ammonite?' he asked.

He picked it up and examined it slowly. 'It's a lovely one. Perfect.'

'What's an ammonite, Sir? Is it a stone?'

Jan's table-mates collapsed into giggles. All right, so I wasn't the cleverest person in class.

'It's a fossil.' He perched on my desk, straightening his glasses with his free hand. 'It belongs to the Triassic era, through to the Mesozoic.' Why do teachers do this? I wished the others wouldn't keep twisting round, staring at us. 'It used to be a living creature, this, on the bed of the ocean.' He threw it up in the air and caught it again. 'Millions of years old this is, James. Imagine that!'

'I thought it was a stone,' I said.

The Jan mob giggled again.

'People used to call it a snake-stone, because they thought it was a petrified snake. Lovely specimen.' He handed it back to me. 'Did you find it?'

'My mother gave it to me,' I said. I put it carefully back next to the notebook. He stayed there, watching me, and eventually the others settled back to their work. In three minutes the bell would go. I flicked through the road atlas.

'Planning a half-term holiday?' the Griffin asked.

'I'm just trying to find somewhere,' I said, 'but it's a bit hard.'

'I see.' He glanced at my notebook and seemed to take it all in. He eased himself into the chair next to me and slid the book towards him. 'Well, let's look at the big map of Britain.' He flicked open the atlas to the first page, where Britain was laid out in its familiar poodle shape. 'I love maps, don't you?'

He loved maps! Bits of paper with names dotted on! I cleared my throat, caught Digger's eyes, and swopped a grin.

'Think of the rivers and valleys and mountains spread out here,' the Griffin went on dreamily. 'Think of the motorways speeding with cars! And the railways throbbing with trains. All the cities and towns and …'

'I'm actually looking for this place,' I reminded him, showing him my notebook. Everyone was looking round again. 'Something Cottage.'

'Start at the bottom. … yshire. What do you notice?'

'I don't know.' I gazed at the map. It was all a maze of blue and red and yellow lines.

'You're looking for a county. I have a feeling that there's only one county in Britain ending in "yshire". Know what it is?'

The bell rang, to my relief. He stood up.

'Er …' he said loudly to the class, and they all sank back into their chairs. 'A table at a time, please! Come to the staff room at the end of the afternoon and I'll lend you an OS map,' he told me.

I stayed at my desk, twisting the atlas round to look at all the shire county names that were printed in pale grey across it. 'Got it!' I said at last, loud with excitement.

The classroom was empty.

After school I hurried down to the staff room. I wanted to go trampolining that evening for ground practice. That meant I'd need an early meal. I ran across the yard from the science labs but even then I nearly didn't make it. I was stopped by Pieface Mygrove, who put his hand on my head and pressed down as if he was trying to shove me through the concrete. Digger was behind him, grinning at me as if he was still my friend.

'Hi,' he said.

I waved my arms about and Pieface pressed down harder.

'Digger's been telling me about your precious stone,' Pieface said. 'Let's see it.'

'No way.' I grunted into my collar bone. My heart was thudding. 'Leave off, Lestor. I've got to see Mr Griffiths.'

Pieface just pressed harder. My nose was somewhere round his belly button. I kicked out and he buckled back, pretending to laugh at me. Then he lunged his hands into my pockets before I had a chance. He brought out the ammonite and held it up away from me, whistling.

'Is this it?' he asked Digger. 'A bit of old stone?'

'It's very old, the Griffin said,' Digger told him.

Meanwhile I was leaping up and down trying to pull Pieface's arm down to my level.

He backed away from me, holding his arm above his head. 'Could be worth a lot of money, something like this,' he said.

I swung my sportsbag at Pieface's belly and winded him. He gasped and then chuckled down at me.

'Did you want something?'

'Bus!' Digger shouted suddenly. He picked up his bag and sprinted down to the gate, where the school bus was just beginning to pull away. Pieface winked at me, turned to follow him, and flipped the ammonite back over his shoulder without saying anything. I only just caught it.

I raced off to the staff room, twisting round to make sure

55

Pieface was on the bus. He waved at me from the top deck as it pulled away.

The Griffin had obviously forgotten his promise, but he covered up well. I suppose teachers are used to doing that. He was pushing his bike out of the staff room door when I arrived and he just raised his hand in a salute when he saw me, passed his bike over for me to hold, and backed in again. He returned with a pile of yellow Ordnance Survey maps.

'Which one d'you want, then?' he asked me.

'Derbyshire,' I said proudly.

'White Peak or Dark Peak?'

He laughed at my puzzled expression. 'Limestone or sandstone? That's how the Peak District's divided. Here, take the big tourist map of Derbyshire. That should do you. Any particular reason why you're interested?'

'I was born there, Sir.' I didn't put the map into my sportsbag. I tucked it down inside my sweatshirt. Silly, really. It was only a map. But like my ammonite and my Sammy note, it belonged to my unknown past.

Notes for Chapter 7

Elizabeth tells us more about her 'wild boy' and her happiness at being with him. James competes at a local diving competition. We learn more about how he came to take up diving. As he dives, he loses concentration when he becomes aware that a woman is watching him. His preoccupation with his birth mother makes him feel that this could be her. As a result he dives poorly, which upsets his father.

What do you think?
In this chapter the author tells us more about both Elizabeth's and James' past experiences. As you read, think about:
- what Elizabeth's memories tell us about her home life
- what James' memories tell us about the attitude of his parents to his diving.

Questions
1. Why do you think the way James gets on with his fellow competitors differs from the way he gets on with the other pupils at his school?
2. Why do you think James' diving upsets his mother?
3. James' father seems to be more upset at James' failure to win than James is. Why do you think he takes James' diving so seriously?

Further activity
Now that you are becoming familiar with a number of the main characters, start to make a character chart for each of them. Each chart should be have four columns headed *Key Point*, *Comment*, *Quotation* and *Page*.

Key Point	Comment	Quotation	Page

In the column headed *Key Point*, you should include details such as appearance, what she or he does, what others say about him/her or do to him/her, and so on. In the second column, put a brief comment about what this tells you about the character and how she or he might be changing. Where possible, put a brief, appropriate quotation from the text in the third column, with a page reference in the fourth column so you can quickly find the place when you want to check back.

Chapter 7

I kept thinking about the wild boy, that night on the tor.

He came in the summer with his people in their vans and caravans. Camped in my uncle's fields and wouldn't go away, even though Uncle Staff and Father used to go down there shouting at them and running their tractors at the animals. Set their stubby grey horses to cropping the grass as if it was their proper home. Made my father swear, that did.

I used to hear the wild people singing at night. Saw the camp-fires glowing.

I loved them. I loved the wild people. They were happy.

When the wild boy saw me looking from the trees he laughed at me. Made me laugh – sweet, sweet laugh.

'What you called?' he asked me.

Everyone in the valley knows my name. They just know it without asking. Made me blush to tell him.

'Elizabeth,' I said. Sounded strange, saying it like that.

'Elizabeth.' Nice the way he said it.

I laughed then. 'Tell yours'.

'Sam,' he said.

'Go on!' I said. 'My father's called that. Samuel, they call him. He's not like you though, Father isn't.'

I miss Sam, I do. In my dreams I miss him.

That weekend I had to dive at a local meet. It was a county championship and it would be a qualifier for the Nationals. Dad came with me, as usual, and Mum came

59

part of the way and went to spend the day with Rachel. I missed Matt. We would have had a good time in the hostel the night before, seeing how many puddings we could get through. Poor old Matt, I kept thinking. I'd rather he was here with me any day, jossing with me in the showers, nicking my towel, giving me serious lectures about girls; even winning the cup. If only he lived nearer I would have gone to see him, but what with school and training I never had a spare minute. Besides, I was a bit shy about going to his house.

Dad stayed with the other coaches in an hotel and I shared a hostel room with three other lads. I had to keep my contact lenses in an egg cup because I'd forgotten the holder. One of the lads was the worst snorer I've heard in my life. He sounded like a motorbike that kept backfiring; pop, pop, pop every few minutes. Just when you thought it was safe to drift off to sleep again he would start up his popping. We ended up piling all our pillows on top of his face. It was well past midnight before any of us slept. I didn't bother writing that down in my diving log. Coach would have written 'You must get plenty of sleep before competitions' next to it. Try telling that to the motorbike.

The only trouble with these competitions is that unless you're good at Maths you don't know how well you're doing until they've finished all the scoring. There's a lot of hanging round to do and some of the divers were very tense because it was their first competition, so no one felt much like talking till after the event. The tension gets to everyone in the end. You rehearse the dives over and over in your head. You can't think about them when you're actually doing them. Just before you leave the board you go over the dive in your head, but you can't stand there forever, you're only allowed a minute, and then you have to go for it. There's a total hush in the pool as you stand there and take your position, arms stretched out, and think about your dive. It's like a prayer, Ken Eldred says. What you daren't think about is the terror of actually leaving the board and travelling through the air at forty miles an hour to the bottom of the pool. You know it's solid. You know how dangerous it is. But diving isn't about danger, it's about difficulty and style.

It wasn't till I took my third jump that I realised I was still wearing my contact lenses. I felt one of them falling out, which unnerved me a bit, but that wasn't a problem. I just hoped I wouldn't end up swallowing it. The real problem came about halfway through the event. I'd done all the set dives and Dad said I was running first. I was actually daydreaming at the time, waiting for my turn for the voluntaries to start, and I was remembering my very first dive, if you could call it that. I was about ten and I was on holiday with Mum and Dad and some friends of theirs. A man taught me how to dive in from the side instead of just holding my nose and jumping in any old how. I was scared and had to be coaxed in, but I went with my hands first and head down and I'll never forget that first entry, with the feel of the water streaming and bubbling round my face and my ears. I came up yelling my head off. As soon as I'd climbed out I dived in again. I wasn't interested in swimming any more. I just wanted to dive. Then I started noticing the people diving off the high boards. I lay on my back and watched them for ages and I knew I wanted to be up there. On the last day of the holiday I made myself climb up to the ten metre board. I just sat on it for ages, hugging my knees, with my stomach churning over and over. I think the others all forgot about me. I knew I wouldn't be climbing back down those steps, but this time there was no one egging me on or laughing or counting me down. No one would even know if I did it or not. It was all inside me, the will to do it, churning tight and hot, mixed up with the fear that pitched about in the pit of my stomach. And then all of a sudden I just did it. I just went to the end of the board and kind of rolled off. I think that was the greatest achievement of my life.

'Number 7. James Logan.' My number was called for the last dive of the first round. I'd chosen a simple inward dive with pike. Dead clean; I loved it. Ken always reckoned the simple dives showed off a diver's real talent. I climbed up, stepped forward to the end of the board, turned, and stood with my heels just balancing over the edge. Steady. I stretched out my arms to the sides. Then I swung up my arms, piked down, and extended out of it without a splash. It was a peacher.

When my number was called for the second round I was day-dreaming about all the medals and cups we've got at home, and I was thinking that nothing, not even if one day I fulfilled my private dream and won the Olympic Gold – not even that would be as exciting as the day I had won my very first competition. It was only a local meet about a year after I'd joined the diving club and we were in the usual state of not knowing how the scoring had gone and by that time not caring, all giggling and shivering in a bunch at the back of the pool. The scores were announced, and mine was the highest. I heard Dad give a whoop from the balcony. I remember that I couldn't stop grinning. I was given the medal and a handshake from the mayor and then I raced up the balcony steps to show my medal to Mum and Dad and Rachel. I couldn't stop grinning and Mum couldn't stop crying. She never came to a competition again – she said it upset her too much. Even then I wasn't really ambitious as a diver. I just loved it so much that I couldn't think of anything else. It was Dad who wanted the triumphs.

'James Logan.' Dad nudged me out of my daydream and I ran up the steps again.

My next dive was a forward two-and-a-half somersault in piked position, and it was another peacher. I knew my scoring would be good. I climbed out and waited for my turn to come again, and that was when things began to go wrong.

I knew that someone was watching me intently. It was a woman sitting on her own. She was leaning forward, very interested, and every time I looked up I could tell, even in my one-eyed state, that she was watching me as if she couldn't take her eyes off me. I tried to be casual. I kept blowing my hands and rubbing my hair as if I hadn't noticed anything, but all the same I began to feel prickly with nerves. My name and number were called again and I ran up the steps too fast. I was heaving for breath by the time I got to the top. I wished she wasn't watching me. I went to the edge of the board and balked. I went back to the steps and tried to breathe steadily. It wasn't that I was scared. I couldn't concentrate on anything except the thought of that woman way below me with hair that was as black as mine; shiny, bluey damsony black such as I'd never seen before except in my mirror. I positioned myself and this time I went for it, but I dived like a goldfish in a trance, just about making it look right.

'For God's sake, concentrate,' Dad whispered when I joined him again. 'Concentrate, concentrate!'

Perhaps she had been following my diving career. I'd had my photograph in the paper lots of times, grinning my head off, holding up a trophy or a medal. And now she couldn't keep away. She had to come and see me for herself. That would be why she was sitting at the back, hoping she wouldn't be noticed. And now she'd seen me at my worst.

I climbed up for my next dive with dread like concrete weights holding down my legs. My best dive was to come. A reverse one-and-a-half somersault with tuck. It was a hard one for me because I much preferred going off the board backwards. I'd been building up to it for weeks. I'd dreamed it every night. I'd done it perfectly in the warm-up that morning. She had to see this one. I even glanced in her direction before I ran along the board, kind of dedicating it to her. It threw me off balance, that glance. Even as I left the board I knew I'd rushed the take-off. I compensated by tucking in tighter than I would have done usually but my entry was bad and splashy and I knew I'd be heavily marked down for it. I climbed out and sat by Dad with my head in my hands, and didn't even move when the scores were announced. I'd come fourth. Dad said nothing. I stood up just as the woman was coming towards me. I felt shaky. Surely she wasn't going to speak to me in front of Dad? However many times I'd fantasised about meeting my real mother I had never imagined it would happen in front of Mum or Dad. This was all wrong.

'Well done, James,' she said, smiling at me. 'I quite liked your style.' Then she walked past me to talk to the boy who'd come first.

'You muffed that all right,' Dad said.

'Sorry.' I was still staring after her.

'That woman is looking for a kid to make a commercial for swimming costumes. Just think of the money you'd have made if she'd picked you.'

'I wish you'd told me,' I said.

'I didn't want to put you off your stroke,' Dad said. 'But I might as well have done for all the good you did up there. I've seen a stuffed salmon do a better dive than that last one. You really let me down.'

'Dad! Everyone's listening.'

'Serves you right if everyone is listening. What the hell were you thinking about?'

'My mother, if you must know.'

I don't know whether he understood me or not. I didn't really care.

Notes for Chapters 8 and 9

Elizabeth finds that her feelings towards her baby are changing. James plans a journey to discover his birth mother. Under the pretence of going on a training week, he sets off to the Peak District.

What do you think?
James deliberately sets out to deceive his parents so that he can search out his past. As you read, think about:
- whether James is justified in his deception
- how each of his parents feels differently about James going away on his own.

Questions
1. What happens to make Elizabeth's feeling towards her child change?
2. Does James' methodical planning of his search surprise you?
3. How does James' mother show her love both for James and her husband in these chapters?
4. What do you think James is feeling as his lies and deceptions grow?

Further activity
James has to take many factors into account when planning his journey. Imagine you are going on holiday to a place some distance away which you have chosen, and your parents have asked you to prepare a plan for them which shows all the details of the journey. Choose your destination and plan your journey. You will need to make a number of important decisions, for example:
- where you are going to travel to
- how you will travel – road, rail, air or sea, or a combination of some of these
- the clearest way to present your information.

When you have decided on your route, you should work out the likely costs.

Make a table to show the information. You may find it helpful to look at the way in which bus and rail timetables are set out, but remember that they usually include far more information than you will require.

Chapter 8

Great-grandfather's donkey path started just past the bridge. Glad of it, but the stones were slippery with wet. They gleamed white like faces in the black ground.

Hard to walk, holding that bundle against me. Mam's funeral coat made me hot, except for my hands. Couldn't feel my hands no more.

Bob slouching, wanting home. So did I. We were way up, never been as far as this. First grouse woke up just under my feet, clattered loud enough to crack my ears open.

Go back, go back, she cackled.

Don't worry. Wanted to. Wanted to go back to last year, before all this happened, and Mam still alive.

Light came slow and lazy. Made me feel better. Dark was lonely, scary a bit.

But light brought more sleet. Cold, even in Mam's coat. Couldn't stop shivering, and that woke the little thing up. Heard it crying in its bundle.

More it cried, more I wanted to look at it. Just to see. Mustn't look at it. Mustn't know it's real.

But I did look. Stopped near the top of the Tor. Sky grey as smoke. Too cold, too sore, too tired to go on. Huddled behind boulders, like the sheep do. Looked inside the bundle.

Black hair, like the wild boy.

A boy baby.

I don't know why I didn't tell Mum and Dad what I was

thinking of doing. If I had told them they'd have asked me to wait until I was older, probably. They might even have wanted to help me. I didn't want to hurt Mum's feelings in any way. It wasn't a criticism of her. But I didn't want to share it with her, or with anybody. It was to do with my real self, and it was a secret, private thing. So I just decided to do it. It was a bit like the moment when I rolled off the high board, all by myself.

So I handed Mum's road atlas back to her without saying anything and I went up to my room with the Griffin's tourist map. I pushed a chair against the door, and I opened up the map on my bed with my ammonite on one side of it and my Sammy note on the other. Derbyshire was huge, with lots of brown contour lines to show how hilly it was. I remembered the Griffin's advice and looked at the next clue from the bottom … lygate. I was absolutely methodical about it. I cut a square out of a piece of paper and used it as a window to slide over the map. That way I looked at every single place name on it in turn. And at last I found it, and there was only one thing it could possibly be. Hollygate. It was so easy. It was like a good omen, the fact that it had been so easy. One county, one town. It was then that I knew for sure what I was going to do. I suppose I had always known really, from the moment that familiar word 'adopted' had jumped like a stranger off the page at me. It had never stopped banging about in my head since then. I had to find her.

I put the map and the Sammy note and the ammonite in

the drawer under my bed. Half-term was the week after next. I went downstairs and told Mum and Dad.

'You know that idea you had about sending me to London for a week's training at half-term?' I said, casual as a cat.

'Oh yes?' said Mum. 'Thought about it, have you?'

'I'd like to do it,' I said. I don't think I'd ever lied to her before. My face felt as if it was on fire.

Chapter 9

When I'd seen him, I wanted him to live. That were all I could think about.

Tried to keep him warm, snuggled in my coat, the way Mam used to bring Uncle Staff's new lambs home when their mothers had died.

Not frighted then. Not after I'd seen him.

'Can I buy my own ticket?' I asked when we got to the station. I was very nervous. After all, the only thing I knew for certain was that I wasn't going to London.

'No,' said Dad. 'I want to pay by credit card, so I have to do it.'

Mum saw my disappointment. She does spoil me, Mum does. I think she tries to make up for not spending much time with me.

'He's a young man now, he wants to do things like this for himself.' She smiled at me as if I was taking my first baby step towards independence. I suppose I was, really. 'Let him.'

'I've no cash!' Dad was impatient with her.

Mum pulled out some cash from her bag and handed it to me, saying nothing. Then she linked her arm in Dad's. 'Come on, Pedro. I'll treat you to a coffee while we're waiting.'

His name is Peter but she always calls him Pedro when he's in a mood. I don't know how, but it seems to get him out of it. So off they went, actually laughing about something secret that she whispered to him, and that's how I managed to buy my own ticket. I was as wily as a fox that week.

I ran over to the ticket booths before they had a chance to follow me. The woman behind the barrier was half asleep.

'I want to go to Derbyshire,' I said, very fast and as loud as I dared. She tortoised her head out of a yawn.

'Derby. When are you coming back?'

'Derby? I don't think I want Derby. It's a place called Hollygate.'

'Never heard of it,' she said.

'Near Chapelfield.'

'Oh, Chesterfield.'

'Not Chesterfield. Please. Chapelfield. Hollygate?' I looked along the line to see if I could go to any of the other booths but they all had queues. The woman yawned again, long and windy, with her eyes going oozy with sleep. Fancy having a mother like that, I thought.

'Never heard of either of them.'

She swivelled away from me, and I was in despair I can tell you, expecting Dad to come up behind me any second. I realised then that she was peering at a computer screen. She took for ever. People behind me were fidgeting and muttering. I glanced round, hoping I couldn't be seen from the coffee bar. If Dad thought I was having difficulties buying my ticket he'd be over like a shot.

'Change at Manchester,' the woman said at last. 'When you coming back, love?'

'Are you sure that's right?' I asked anxiously. 'I don't think Manchester's in Derbyshire.'

'It's as near as dammit,' the man behind me in the queue said. 'How long are you going to keep this up? I'm about to miss my train.'

I looked round again, saw Dad sauntering over to a newspaper stand, and shoved Mum's money into the little turnstile bucket. 'I don't know when I'm coming back,' I said.

The woman creased her face into a yawn again and piled my tickets and a load of returned money into the bucket. I crammed it all into the back pocket of my jeans, trying not to feel guilty. One day, I thought, I'd return it to Mum.

Dad waved to me and came over. 'She took her time,' he said. 'How much?'

'Erm … just about what Mum gave me,' I said. I told you I was getting wily that week. 'Can I keep the change for a drink on the train?'

'You've got your packed lunch,' he reminded me. Mum joined us and gave me a bar of wholenut chocolate, my favourite.

Somehow I persuaded them not to see me off from the platform. I told them I wanted to go to the toilet first.

'You can go on the train,' Dad pointed out. 'Don't miss it, for goodness sake. You've only got about five minutes.'

'Don't fuss, Pedro,' Mum said, and immediately started smoothing down the sticky-up bit of my hair.

'Have you got your contact lens stuff?'

'I'll phone you tonight at Uncle James's,' I told them. I knew this would start problems. 'And you can give me your hotel number for the rest of the week.'

'Don't be ridiculous,' Dad said. 'You'll be spending all your pocket money on phone calls.'

'I'd rather do it,' I said. If Ken Eldred told them I hadn't turned up they'd be setting up a police search straight away.

'Let him, Pedro,' Mum said. She opened her bag again and gave me a phone card. 'There's plenty left on that, James. As long as you do phone, mind.'

'Make it after six,' Dad said, 'when it's cheaper.' He looked miserable. It was the first time I'd been away without him. I felt pretty miserable too. I'd never deceived them before. I'd never had to. Mum was making it so easy for me.

'I'll have to go,' I said. I went to hug Mum and I felt choked. I felt as if I'd never see her again. She rocked me backwards and forwards, upsetting herself, upsetting us both. I didn't have to do it, I thought. Not if it hurt her.

'Off you go,' she said. 'Enjoy yourself.'

I picked up my sportsbag, shook hands with Dad, which felt really strange, and ran over the bridge for the London train.

I was wily. I did not know until then how wily I could be, or how guilty it would make me feel. I actually did get on the London train, with a minute to spare. I sat on the side nearest to the bridge, just in case Mum and Dad had taken it into their heads to watch the train go from the far platform. Then I pretended to discover that the seat had a reserve ticket on the back. I jumped up and took my bag from the rack and moved to stand near the door just as a guard was slamming it shut. I can't believe it now, but I actually waited until the whistle was blown, then I flung open the door and belted out on to the platform. By this time my heart was prancing about like a wildcat inside me. I dived for the men's toilets. It was five minutes before I dared to come out again. There was no sign of them.

This was where my real bit of wiliness came in. I rang Ken Eldred. This was going to be difficult, because I'd spoken to him the night before and he had a brilliant training programme set up for me. I think I was one of his rising stars, actually. It would have been a fantastic week. I was dreading letting him down.

As it happened, it was his wife who answered the phone. She looks after Ken's divers like a chirpy sparrow, fussing round us all and making sure we eat enough when we stay there. She never eats herself. She's bony and fidgety and smoke piles out of her mouth when she talks.

'James, dear!' she twittered. 'Kenny's over in the gym. Shall I take him a message?'

That was perfect. By the time she got my message to Ken she'd have forgotten half of it and he'd be annoyed with her, not with me. Even so, my wiliness was making me sweat. I was a hopeless liar. I tried to keep as near to the truth as possible.

'I'm just ringing to let him know I'm going to be a bit late,' I said.

'Oh dear. Missed your train?'

'A couple of days late, actually. My friend's just come out of hospital, and I want to go up to his place and see him before I come to London.'

'Oh dear, is he very poorly? Oh, and you'll miss all that coaching! Isn't it good of you to put your friend first!'

'His parents are going to Scotland, you see,' I plunged in deeper.

'Straight after he's come out of hospital? Well, that's not very nice …'

'Well, his mother's not going … but she'll be out at work … she works Saturdays and Sundays …' The sound of a whistle brought me to my senses. 'I'll have to get my train, Bette. Tell Ken I'll see him in a couple of days.'

'Try to do your press-ups every day …'

I hung up on her warbling, picked up my bag, and headed for the Manchester train. As soon as it started moving I began to relax. I put my hand in my pocket and snugged the ammonite into my palm. I was going to find my mother.

Notes for Chapters 10 and 11

James continues his journey, but finds that he cannot reach his destination except on foot. The weather turns wet and he accepts a lift to the nearby youth hostel. The following day, after an unexpected encounter with Pieface Mycroft, he reaches Hollygate. Elizabeth too has reached Hollygate and reluctantly leaves her baby in a posting box outside a cottage, leaving a brief note on the torn-off corner of an envelope.

What do you think?
Not everything in James' journey goes according to plan. He is aware of how he is letting down people he loves and values. As you read, think about how James responds to:
- the news of Matt's improvement
- the cancellation of his train
- his encounter with Pieface.

What new information tells you that James' search for his birth mother's home will be harder than he thinks?

Questions
Look for words and phrases to help you to answer these questions:
1. How are we made aware that James dislikes lying to people?
2. How does James' behaviour during his journey support his feeling that he is possessed?
3. What tells us that Elizabeth's attitude to her baby has changed?
4. Why does James agree to buy his snake-stone back from Pieface?

Further activity
Many people make collections, sometimes of quite strange things, often of little monetary value like fossils, but treasured by their owners. Prepare a talk on making a collection, either your own or a friend's. Consider: why the collection was started; how long it has taken to build up the collection; special items in the collection; the collector's favourite pieces.

When you present your talk, try to have some items or pictures to show your audience.

Chapter 10

At Manchester I was told to wait for a connection. I was beginning to feel bad about all the lies I'd been telling. The thing about grown-ups is that they can just go where they want or do what they want without having to tell lies about it. I had to account for every minute of my day to someone. I decided to make up for it by ringing up Matt's parents. His mother was really pleased to hear from me. She took the phone to Matt and he said he was fed up with having to stay in bed for most of the time. It was strange talking to him on the phone. I felt very awkward.

'When will you be diving again?' I asked him.

He went quiet, and I thought he must have dropped the receiver.

'Matt?'

'I don't know … Mum's not keen.'

'Oh. Right.' I felt as glum as he sounded. 'She'll come round to it.'

'Yeah. You diving at the weekend?'

'Don't know,' I said. 'I'm supposed to be …'

'Two-and-a-half reverse summy. Do the two-and-a-half reverse, James. Go for it!'

His voice sounded croaky. I pushed my fist against the sides of the phone booth. The glass was cold and hard, like the surface of a pool from far up.

'Have to go,' I said. 'Train to catch.'

'Yeah,' he said. His voice kept coming and going. It was a terrible line. 'Thanks for ringing, James. It was good.'

It was good. It was great to hear him. And it made me feel a bit better about all those lies.

My train was delayed by ten minutes, then thirty, then forty, then cancelled altogether. I ate my sandwiches and fed the crusts to the station pigeons. It was amazing how many of them had toes missing. I wondered if people kept standing on them or whether they got them trapped in the escalator or bitten off by other pigeons mistaking them for crusts. I felt really sorry for them and did my best to give my biggest crusts to the toeless ones.

I was quite happy sitting there in the sunshine watching people coming and going. A down-and-out came wandering along asking people for money. The only change I had was 10p and I thought that might offend him so I didn't give it to him. Actually I felt embarrassed at the thought of giving money to a grown-up. It was the wrong way round. He did look hungry, though. I suppose the best thing I could have done was to have given him my sandwiches, but I'd eaten most of those and the pigeons had eaten the rest. I could have just left them on the bench for him so it didn't look like charity. But then the station police might have thought it was a suspicious parcel and blown it up. Scrambled egg and chutney, they were. They'd have made quite a mess. Anyway, I'd eaten them.

I tried not to watch him and watched the women instead, imagining that one of them was my mother and that she'd come to Manchester for a day's shopping. I was always imagining I saw her. I only ever saw my father on diving championships on television. He was always the winner. But I saw my mother everywhere I went. I only looked at the women who were without children. If my mother had given me away she would hardly have gone and had any more, would she?

Then I saw a tall woman with bluey-black hair like mine. She was like the woman in the swimming pool but very much smarter. Rich, I'd say, and very beautiful. She was looking round her as if she was waiting for someone. It could be her. I'd been so lucky with the clues so far that it could easily be her. I had to speak to her. What if she got into a taxi and drove away and I never saw her again? All my life I'd be wishing I'd spoken to her. So I slung my bag over my shoulder and sauntered across to her and tried to look casual, but in my nervous state my feet shuffled along like a pigeon's. The nearer I got to her the harder I found it to look at her. I stopped right by her, willing her to look at me. She had to recognise me. I could smell her perfume.

'Excuse me ...' I blurted out. 'I'm –'

I'm what?

Her eyes slid past me as if I didn't really exist. She raised her hand slightly as if she was trying to push away the air between us. 'Sorry,' she said, and walked quickly away, casting me off. I knew then how the down-and-out felt.

I almost missed my train when it was announced.

I was actually practising toe-pushes by the bookstand and I'd begun to forget that I was supposed to be waiting for the train. I ran through a flapping cloud of pigeons and just caught it. I flopped down on to the seat and blew out my cheeks. Another hour to get there. And then what?

I arrived at last at a small higgledy-piggledy town that seemed to fall away down a steep hillside. It was past five in the afternoon by then. Outside the station I asked a woman the way to Hollygate.

'Bit far,' she said. 'About six or seven miles, love.'

'Where do I get the bus?' I asked.

'Bus?' the woman laughed. 'There's no bus or train from here to Hollygate. You'll have to go by Shanks's pony.'

'I've never ridden a pony,' I told her, and she seemed to think this was a great joke.

'Never heard of Shanks's pony? Them's your legs – though who Shanks was or is I haven't a clue.'

She put her hand under my elbow and steered me to the edge of the pavement. 'Go to the end of the road,' she said. 'Turn left, and then just follow the signposts. You'll be there in a couple of hours, big strong lad like you.'

Of course I'm not big. I'm skinny. I eat more than anyone else in our class and I'm tons fitter and I still look a good year younger than any of them. That's why I don't get anywhere with girls like Jan. 'Think tall,' Ken always says. 'Make yourself go for full stretch all the time.' You pull in your stomach and your bottom muscles. That gives you a few inches straight away. I still looked skinny.

I obediently followed the way the woman pointed. When I got to the corner I turned round and she was still watching me, her arms on her hips, her feet planted wide each side of her as if she had taken root. What if it's her, I thought, and banished the idea from my mind. I waved to her. I wanted her to go away. As soon as I turned round the corner I sat on the kerbstone. I wasn't ready to go any further yet. I needed to think.

Six miles was a long way, but it was also very near. I was six miles away from seeing the place where I was born – possibly six miles away from seeing my mother. I took out the crumpled Sammy note again, and turned it over. 'se cottage'. I wondered how many cottages there would be in Hollygate. If it was the same size as the place I'd just come to there could be a few hundred. They wouldn't all end in 'se' though. What could it be? Rose Cottage. It was the only one I could think of. It had to be that. And what on earth would I do when I found it? Knock on the door? Say 'Hi. I'm your long-lost son!' and expect her to give me a hug and invite me in for a toasted teacake? Ask me to forgive her? Was that what I wanted? I didn't really know what I wanted. I think I just wanted to know what she looked like, that was all. Just so I could believe she was a real person.

And there was another worry. Where was I going to sleep that night? I hadn't really thought beyond making this visit to Hollygate. I'd had no idea it would take me so long to get this far. Maybe I half-imagined I'd be sleeping in my mother's cottage, in a room with beams across the ceiling and flowery wallpaper. But now that I was so near to finding her I knew for certain that I wouldn't give up until I had, even if it took the whole week. All I had with me was my swimming gear, one change of clothes and the sleeping bag I always took to Ken and Bette's. So I might have to sleep under a hedge. I thought of the down-and-out. I bet he did that every night. And it was a lovely sunny evening. I quite liked the idea.

But it would take me two to three hours to walk to Hollygate. If I didn't phone before six Dad would be bound to ring Ken Eldred in London. That would be disastrous. And there might not be a phone box on the way, or it might have been vandalised. I walked back to the station and waited outside the phone booth there. It didn't take phone cards. I dashed into a shop and bought a can of coke to get change, and then I thought about the night under the hedge and bought some peanuts and some chocolate. That was another wily move. I had to queue again to use the phone. I dialled Uncle James's number, planning my story in my head. It was the ansafone. I hate the things usually but that day it was brilliant. The last person I wanted to have to speak to was Mum.

'Hi,' I said. 'It's James. Tell Mum and Dad I got here safely. Bye.'

I felt liberated. Not a single lie, if they didn't stop to wonder where 'here' meant. I came out into the sunshine, swung my bag over my shoulder, and set off at a jog down the lane to Hollygate.

Proper morning by the time we walked into that other valley. Could hear tractors and cars. Bits of snow flittering round me.

Saw a house with its lights on. Stopped and hid. Watched a woman coming out scattering bread on her path.

When she went back in I went down the track to her gate. Nice, posh house it was, not like ours. There was a box by the gate, for the letters. Green, wooden box, with a lift-up lid.

Think the baby was asleep, all snug in his sack. I put the baby in the box.

Underneath the box was a crate for milk bottles, and a torn envelope, and a pencil dangling from a string. There was a message on the paper – 'no milk today'.

I tore a piece off the envelope. Didn't know what to say. Didn't know what to call him, even. Can't leave him without giving him a name.

Then I thought of the wild boy.

I must have been going for just over an hour when it started to rain. The weather changed completely from being a sunny afternoon to a grey and glowering evening, and it was pouring. It didn't just drizzle; it came in great wallowing waves, dredging down my collar and into my pockets and trainers. I could have swum in it. I sheltered underneath a tree that had so many gaps in it might as well have been a waterfall. I was too miserable to try to go on. It looked as if the rain was in for the night. I unzipped my sportsbag and took out my towel, which I draped over my head. It helped for a bit. My teeth were chattering and my hands were red and numb. And I don't know where the thought came from but I suddenly realised that I still didn't have the phone number of the hotel that Mum and

Dad were going to with Uncle James. At this very minute Dad might be phoning Ken Eldred to leave him a message about it. But to tell the truth I was so wet that I didn't even care.

I ripped open the bag of peanuts and started cramming them into my mouth, wretched with myself because I'd meant them to last for breakfast as well as tea, but even so I didn't stop eating them till I'd finished the whole packet, and then I felt so thirsty that I drank the can of coke. I was about to start on the chocolate too, telling myself that I needed it for comfort, when a Land Rover drew up with a man and woman in it.

'D'you want a lift anywhere?' the woman called. 'You look wet through, lad.'

The Land Rover was pointing back the way I'd come. The thought of getting a train back home was very welcoming. Anyway, how could I present myself to my long-lost mother looking like that? I hesitated. I was really tempted to just give up.

'You're miles from anywhere,' the man said. 'Come on. In you get.'

The branch above my head turned upside down and emptied itself down the back of my neck. That decided me. I slid in thankfully, stuffing my soaked towel in my bag. I squeezed in next to the woman, who smelt so strongly of fried onions and sausages that I could have eaten her coat.

'Where d'you live?' the man asked. 'I've not seen you around before.'

This could be a trick question. They might just have heard on the news about a boy who'd gone missing. 'I'm on holiday,' I said truthfully. 'I was just going for a walk.'

'Oh, from the youth hostel, are you?'

The youth hostel. I swallowed hard, and let my head roll back. I'd stayed in youth hostels on school trips and sometimes during competition meets. There'd be food, a hot shower, a bed, a drying room. It was the answer to a vagrant's prayer, and I still had plenty of change left from Mum's money. This was worth a lie. 'Yes,' I said. 'The YHA.'

'We'll drop you there,' the woman said. 'It's a good walk once you get to the lane, Bill.'

After about a mile along the road I'd just come down we swung up a badly rutted lane that flung us all from side to side. At the end of the drive was a long, barn-like building with lots of windows, and the lights from it glowed through the gloom. I thanked the couple and tipped myself out again into the rain.

The warden said I could stay for a night without joining the YHA, and I paid up thankfully for a hot meal, in spite of all the peanuts, and an overnight stay with breakfast. Then I looked for the phone. I rang Uncle James, dreading what I might hear.

'Hello there, James!' my uncle said. 'They've just arrived. Hang on, I'll get your dad.'

The car had broken down on the way, Dad said. It had taken them hours to get there. He was flustered and hungry and not in the mood for talking. 'Sounds as if you're ringing from the pool,' he said, as a couple of boys ran past, yelling at each other in the echoey room. 'Have a good time, James.'

'Thank you,' I said, as I put the receiver back on its cradle. 'Thank you for everything, James Alexander Bell.'

I had a shower and changed into my dry clothes and put everything else I possessed into the boiler room to dry. The place was steaming with damp clothes. Then I munched my way through two helpings of a massive hostel meal, listening to the ramblers' tales of the people round me, and almost nodded off into my third bowl of rice pudding. Two cyclists arrived late and we could all hear the hostel warden making a great joke about the fact that there would have been enough food for them if one of the hostellers hadn't scoffed all the left-overs. The people on my table had a laugh at my expense. Normally I would have joined in. But I knew one of the cyclists. My stomach went stone cold at the sound of his high-pitched laugh out in the hall. I sneaked out and up the stairs, and from the top landing I leaned down to make sure. It was Pieface Mygrove.

I went straight to the dormitory and got myself a top bunk in the corner away from the door. It was the only one that hadn't been taken, so at least Pieface would be in another room. I decided to stay there and hide. He was the last person I wanted to speak to.

Chapter 11

Next day was bright and sunny. I never even saw Pieface. He must have been self-catering after all, eating in the hostellers' kitchen. Maybe he left early. I actually forgot about him. After my hostel breakfast of porridge and fried eggs and beans on toast I was ready for anything. I was given my chore, which was to sweep out the boys' dormitory. Another boy had been given the same job and it took us ages because he was useless and my brush was bald. At last I was free. I packed all my dry togs back into my sportsbag and swung off down the lane, whistling. I felt terrific. I couldn't wait to be in Hollygate and outside Rose Cottage. I'd never noticed before how nice the countryside was. The hedgerows were full of little flowers all shimmering with dew drops, and the birds were singing louder than a group of schoolkids going wild in a swimming pool.

After half an hour I reached the waterfall tree where I'd tried to shelter the day before. I could hardly believe how miserable and defeated I'd felt then. I felt I could walk for miles now, whatever the weather did. I stopped to take off my jacket. It was just as I was stuffing it into my sportsbag that Pieface and his friend cycled up.

Pieface pulled on his brakes and screeched to a stop. He straddled his bike, grinning at me as if I was his best friend in the whole world.

'I thought I saw you,' he said, 'stuffing your face with porridge.'

I ignored him. My heart was doing slow backwards somersaults.

'This is the school midget,' he told his friend. 'Oh, I forgot, he's also diving champion of the world.' He got off his bike and let it slide to the ground. I straightened up and picked up my sportsbag, and he went for it. He swung it away from me, chuckling. 'And he collects stones, don't you, James?'

He unzipped the bag and tipped out the contents. My ammonite rolled out and before I had a chance to reach it he'd covered it with his size twelve cycling boots.

His friend cycled off slowly, bored or embarrassed. I considered turning my attention to Pieface's bike and demolishing it for him but I knew he'd leave me flattened in a field if I did. I just had to wait to see what his game was. All I knew was that I had to be cool, if I was ever to get my ammonite back. There was no reasoning with a kid like Pieface. After all, there was nothing in his head except gravy.

Pieface picked up the ammonite and looked at it. I could tell he was puzzled by it.

'It's not worth anything, honestly,' I said, as calmly as I could. I was near to retching with panic but I kept myself calm. This is the high dive with no water in the pool, I said to myself. This is a free fall. 'It's just something my mother gave me when I was a kid, that's all.'

'Ah,' he crooned. He whistled to his friend, who came cruising up.

'Ellis, how much would you say this is worth?' Pieface asked him.

Ellis took it from him. 'I dunno. Twenty quid?'

'Sounds fair.' Pieface smiled at me. 'I'll sell it you for eighteen, James. How about that?'

I calculated. I knew I didn't even have that much. 'Ten,' I said. I pulled out the notes and held them towards him. His friend wobbled about on his bike, tossing the ammonite from one hand to the other.

'And the rest,' said Pieface.

'How do I know you'll give it to me?' I asked him.

'Sell it to you,' he corrected.

'I'll make sure you get it,' Ellis promised me. 'I like to see things done properly, I do.'

I emptied out my pockets. I had one more note and a handful of change. Ellis plucked out the note and handed it to Pieface. Then he gave me my ammonite. It was greasy with his sweat. I closed my hands round it.

'You've got a bargain there,' Ellis said.

I closed my eyes. I willed Pieface to go away. I never wanted to see him in my life again. I heard them laughing, heard Pieface picking up his bike, heard them whirring off at last down the lane. I didn't open my eyes again until every shred of the sound of their bikes had gone.

'Look after Sammy', I wrote, careful as anything on the scrap of paper. Sammy. That made him real, giving him a name.

I put the paper next to him in the green box.

He looked so tiny and helpless.

Knew I'd never see him no more.

Wished I had something to give him.

Then I remembered that snake-stone thing in my pocket. It went everywhere with me.

Put it down, gentle as an egg, next to him.

I closed the box lid, and I started to run, fast as I could, holding all the hurt together, belly hurt and crying hurt, all in one.

It was a very long six miles. More like eight. I kept telling myself that I didn't have to go through with it. I could ring Dad's hotel as soon as I got to Hollygate and he'd somehow make it possible for me to get to London. He'd be hurt and angry for what I'd done behind his back, but he'd put my diving first anyway and he'd want to get me back in training. That was all he'd be worried about. And it would be great to be diving again, to spend all day of every day of the holiday getting it right, getting everything perfect for the competition. The more I thought about it, the more I ached to be back on the diving board, keyed up for that free flight through the air.

But I wasn't free any more. I was possessed, wasn't I?

Notes for Chapter 12

James arrives in Hollygate and starts to look for Rose Cottage. But even when he asks directions from a group of local women, he is unsuccessful and is on the point of giving up his quest.

What do you think?
James starts his search for Rose Cottage in the same spirit as he approaches his diving. As you read the chapter, think about:
- how James makes his choice of which woman he is going to speak to
- what his sudden swings of mood tell us about how he feels about what he is doing.

Questions
This is a crucial chapter in the story. James finds the cottage he has been searching for, and makes a new friend.
1. Why does James fix his attention on the woman in the blue dress?
2. Why does James want to avoid having anyone see him discover Rose Cottage?
3. How do we know before he does that James has found the right house?
4. What is significant about Elizabeth's words 'I didn't look back'?

Further activity
Read the last two pages of Chapter 12 again. James has a strange experience which helps him find the cottage he is looking for. Using a dictionary and a thesaurus, look for words which describe such strange experiences. You might start by looking up such words as 'inspiration', 'revelation', 'intuition', etc. Set out your findings in a table of two columns headed *Word* and *Meaning*. Arrange the words in the column headed *Word* in alphabetical order. You may want to use a computer to help you find the words and to set them out in a suitable table.

Chapter 12

Hollygate was a very small village. There were a couple of pubs and a little school and half a dozen shops, a church and a river, and that seemed to be it. The houses were straggled along the main street and up the hill behind it. It wouldn't take long to check them all out. I was beginning to feel very hungry again by now. I stood on the bridge and ate my Mars bar, day-dreaming about diving into the water, which was only about a foot deep. I flexed my shoulders back and felt my stomach muscles tightening, my toes pushing down, my arms light at my side, ready to swing up into position. I thought of Ken and of all his lads diving one after the other, the air snatching at them and cruising them down. Ken expected total commitment from all his divers. After all, he gave it to them. I wondered whether I'd lost my chance for ever with him.

I was hauled away from thinking about all that by the sound of some women laughing. They were standing just by the bridge, outside the post office. My mother could be one of them, I thought. I sat on the bridge watching them, trying to decide which of them I liked best. There was a woman in a blue dress who seemed to be listening calmly to the others without taking part in the conversation herself. She kept glancing over towards me in an amused sort of way as though she thought I was listening in to the conversation, which seemed to be about operations. I liked her. A girl of about my age came to the group and the woman in the blue dress spoke to her and the girl went and sat on the other end of the bridge, staring at me. The other women looked towards me then and I began to feel self-conscious. I went down towards them, swinging my bag casually as I went and almost concussing a small dog that was fastened to one of the women by a long lead. Feeling stupid, I bent down to stroke it and it leapt up at me, just missing my jugular and contenting itself with savaging my jacket with its teeth. All the women shrieked with laughter except for the one in the blue dress, who actually bent down and prised him away from me. I thought she was really nice.

'That dog is a bit of a menace,' she said under her breath. 'Pity you didn't manage to knock him out.'

She began to move away and I went after her, anxious not to be left with the cackling women.

'Can you tell me where Rose Cottage is?' I asked. I was nervous even about saying that. Of all the women there she might be the one. I wanted her to be the one. I hardly dared hope she might be. But she only showed puzzlement in her eyes.

'Rose Cottage?' She had a nice, light voice. 'I don't think there is one in Hollygate, is there?'

'There's a Honeysuckle Cottage,' one of the women said.

'Honeysuckle House,' another one corrected her. 'Though I've only ever seen nettles growing round it.'

'Ivy House.'

'Holly. There's a Holly Cottage. Up behind the church, love.'

I shook my head. 'No. It's definitely Rose Cottage.'

'Sunnydale. Blakeny House. Bridge Cottage …'

They started going through a litany of names, counting on their fingers. The woman in blue smiled at me.

'You don't know who lives there?'

'I think it ends in "m",' I said. '"M" or "on",' I said wretchedly.

'Oh! M!' One of them said. 'Farm. That'll be it. There is a Farm Cottage.'

'White Farm. White Farm Lane!'

'Haven't they sold that place yet?'

'They're thinking of turning it into holiday cottages.'

'It's all right,' I said, willing them to stop. 'I'll ask at the post office.'

'No, you can't!' The woman with the dog was triumphant. 'It's closed!'

'I know what it is!' Another one shouted, rapturous with excitement. 'White Rose Farm! That's what he's looking for! Down at Nether Hollygate.'

The women all turned to me, beaming. I shook my head.

'It doesn't matter,' I said. 'Really and truly it doesn't matter.'

I backed away from them as they all started pointing in different directions. I was sorry I'd asked. I imagined them picking up their shopping bags and the hateful dog and trundling round the village with me, peering at the names on the gates and chuntering on about everyone who lived there.

They were right, though. There was no Rose Cottage in the whole of Hollygate. My feet were sore with trudging, and the warm day had turned to a cool evening by the time I came to that conclusion. I was very hungry, and I had nowhere to go.

'That's it,' I thought. 'I've had enough.' I really had. I decided that the only thing left for me to do was to walk back to the hostel, all eight miles of it. I was sure the warden would let me stay the night there if I promised to get Dad to send him the money next week. And tomorrow I would go home. Home. That was a very inviting word by then. It was an all-forgiving, comfortable word.

The church clock began to strike and I realised that I was an hour late for my phone call. I'd seen a phone box right up at the end of the village. I limped up there. My trainers were giving me blisters. The phone didn't take phone cards, but I had my coins. It took ages for the receptionist at the hotel to put me through to Mum and Dad's room.

'James!' Mum said. It was great to hear her voice. 'We were just about to phone Mr Eldred,' she said. 'You enjoying yourself?'

'Yes,' I said. You've no idea how much I wanted to blurt it all out to her then. The sound of her voice made me feel more homesick than ever. 'Mum, I'm sorry …'

'Are you all right, love? Want to talk to your dad?'

Something outside the phone box was distracting me. It

was like a light blazing through darkness, it was so bright and clear and dazzling. I pushed open the door of the booth to make sure I was seeing it properly.

'James?'

'It's all right, Mum. I'm fine. Great.'

'He's just coming.'

'Can I ring you tomorrow? I've ...'

My money had run out anyway. I put the receiver down in a kind of trance, trying to steady myself, trying to keep my breathing calm. I walked slowly across the lane to the house opposite. The lane ended there, and turned into a dirt track that seemed to go up and up a steep hill, a mountain maybe. The top was in cloud. It was a grey stone house with a long garden full of flowers. There was a milk crate by the gate and a green box on the wall, probably for letters. But it was the name on the gate that blazed across to me.

I was just about to put my hand on the latch when the girl on the bridge sauntered up. I'd forgotten all about her.

'Hi!' she said. 'Found your cottage, then?'

'I got it a bit wrong,' I said. 'It wasn't Rose Cottage.'

'Fancy forgetting a name like this!' she laughed.

Horsenose Cottage. That was it.

I didn't look back. I came to the top of the Tor, and I didn't look back.

White hares were dancing round me.

The blizzard sang in my ears.

Look after Sammy.

Notes for Chapter 13

James finds Horsenose Cottage and meets the girl and her mother whom he had met earlier. He believes he has found his place of birth and his birth mother's house, but soon finds he is mistaken. He agrees to give up his search and go on to London the following day.

What do you think?
James seems to have found his way so far by a series of lucky chances. It is almost as if something is guiding him, and he appears to feel that even his misfortunes are part of the mystery he is unravelling. As you read this chapter, think about how the author keeps us interested by:
- the sudden appearance of Clair at the cottage gate
- the description of how James feels now that he is nearing the end of his quest
- the way in which he finds that once again he is mistaken.

Questions
Find evidence for your answers to these questions by looking at the text:
1. What is James' opinion of his abilities?
2. What differences does James notice between his home and Horsenose Cottage?
3. Why do you think that Clair and James get on so well together?
4. How does Clair's mother manage to prevent James from feeling foolish at his mistake?
5. What does James decide to do in order to find his birth mother?

Further activity
Clair's mother is concerned that James' parents and diving coach will be worried about him. She does her best to persuade him to return to them and to take up his search in a more conventional manner, through an agency which specialises in tracing people. Imagine that you meet someone who is searching for something which is very important to them, but who is going about their search in a manner which you know is mistaken. How would you go about persuading them to try your way, without offending or upsetting them? You could write this as a short story with yourself as one of the characters.

Chapter 13

The girl actually followed me up the path and stood behind me while I rang the bell. She annoyed me. I needed to be on my own for this.

'D'you want something?' I asked her.

'My tea,' she said. 'And it's no good ringing the bell. One's out and the other's in bed.'

'Oh.' I felt completely deflated.

She unlocked the door and I turned away. 'You can come in and wait, if you want,' she said.

So that was how I got into Horsenose Cottage. I gazed round it, wondering which room I'd been born in. It smelt of polish and flowers, and it was old and dark with beams across the ceiling. The walls were covered with paintings of lakes and hills. I wondered whether my mother had painted them. I quite like painting, but I'm not much good at it. I'm not much good at anything except diving.

I followed the girl into the kitchen, which was really old-fashioned and dark. Mum would have called it gloomy, but it was cheered up by a blazing wood fire, even on that June day. I'd never been in a house with a proper fire before, though in the lounge we've got a gas one that pretends to be coal.

'What's your name?' the girl asked me.

'I'd rather not say at the moment.' I don't really know why I said that. It sounded very pompous.

'What did you want to see Mum about?'

I didn't say anything.

'That's a mystery too?'

I nodded.

'Fair enough.' She took some food out of the fridge. 'I don't suppose you'd like some of this, would you? I'm sick to death of cold pizza but Mum says we've got to finish it before we have anything else.'

I tried to look casual. 'I wouldn't mind,' I said. Almost before she'd finished cutting the pizza in half I'd swallowed my share. I could easily have eaten half a dozen pieces that size.

'Haven't you eaten anything today?'

'Not much,' I said.

She leaned back in her chair. 'I know what it is. You've run away from home, haven't you?'

'No. Honestly. I'm on my way to London. I just wanted to look at this place first.'

'This cottage? Why?'

I just couldn't come out with it. It was too important, and it sounded silly. I didn't even know how to say it.

She passed the other half of the pizza across to me. 'You might as well eat this. You'd be doing me a favour, actually.'

'I had my money stolen,' I told her, with my mouth full of pizza.

'I thought it was something like that. So you've come begging!'

'No!' I was alarmed. That was the last thing I wanted anyone to think. 'I've still got some. I came here to … I

102

came here because I wanted to see it again. I've been here before, a long time ago.'

'You'd think you'd remember what it was called then!' she said. 'Horsenose! Stupid name.'

She brought an apple pie out of the fridge, cut it in half, then pushed both pieces towards me and got herself a banana.

'Well,' she said. 'I'm called Clair, even if you haven't got a name. Is that where you live, London?'

I started to explain to her about Ken and my diving. She was really interested. It's the first time a girl has ever been interested in my diving.

'I do Gym,' she said. 'I'm just crazy about Gym. Are you double-jointed?'

I was just starting to demonstrate my diving positions when the door opened and in walked the woman in the blue dress.

She took everything in: me bunched up for a somer-sault; Clair half-way to doing the splits; the empty pizza and apple pie plates; and she just smiled, as I knew she would, and squeezed past us to put away her shopping.

'So you gave up on Rose Cottage,' she said with her back to me.

'He reckons it was this one all the time,' Clair told her, by some miracle hoisting herself back up out of her splits without even putting her hands on the floor. I don't know how she did that. 'And he's been here before, only he couldn't remember the name, and he's had all his money stolen, and he's on his way to London, and Mum … listen! He's a champion diver!'

'I'm sure he can speak for himself,' the nice woman, the mother of my dreams, smiled at me and poured some tea out of the teapot.

'And he's finished off the …'

'Take this cup of tea up for your nan, Clair. She's bound to be awake and gagging for one by now. What's your name?' she asked me, taking me off my guard.

'Believe it or not,' said Clair, 'he hasn't got one.'

And she was gone, leaving me in a terrible state of confusion. Here I was, alone with her at last. Here was the moment I'd dreamed about a hundred million times, and the nice woman in the blue dress smiling at me and waiting for me to speak, and all I could think of, choked in the centre of a whirligig of thoughts, was this: Clair must be my sister.

I sat down at the table, trying to haul my swinging thoughts back into place.

'Well?' The lady in the blue dress sat opposite me at the table and started picking at the apple pie crumbs. 'So you're a mystery visitor.'

'I'm Sammy.'

It came out very easily after all. I didn't blurt it out. I didn't want to shock her. I said it quietly and solemnly, and then I said it again in case she hadn't heard me. I was sure she hadn't, because she just sat there smiling at me still. And because she still didn't register anything I pulled out my precious Sammy note from my pocket and put it on the table in front of her. And then I had to look away from her because all of a sudden it was too much. The silence was killing me. I just wished she'd say something.

I heard her swallowing. She picked up the piece of paper and turned it over in her hand. She stood up and went over to the light, and read both sides. Then she came back to the table. All this seemed to take for ever. Instead of sitting opposite me again she pulled her chair round so she was sitting next to me. She put her arm across the back of my chair so it was almost touching me but not quite. I knew it was there. It was almost burning me.

'I think I understand why you're here,' she said. 'Are you adopted?'

I nodded and cleared my throat.

'Sammy. Look at me.'

I turned my head slightly but couldn't bring myself to look at her, not quite. She was a blur of pink and blue just to the right of my eye.

'I've never seen this note before,' she said.

My hands were clenching and unclenching in my lap. They were actually hurting me. Everything was hurting me. 'But it is this cottage! This is where I was born. There's no other cottage here that's "se" at the end and there's nowhere else in Derbyshire that's "lygate". It has to be Hollygate. And it has to be Derbyshire because … because …'

I heard her laugh slightly. I did look at her then because I thought she must have been laughing at me. She drew her arm away from the back of my chair and clapped her hands together.

'Stop, Sammy! I do believe you! You've done a wonderful piece of detective work to find this house. I'm sure you're right. I wish I could tell you something about this note but I can't.' She pushed her hands through her hair, holding it back from her face as if it helped her to think properly. 'All this must be awfully upsetting for you.'

She moved away from me then and I was glad. I felt as if I'd stopped breathing while she was sitting there. I blew out my cheeks and unclasped my hands at last. She made a lot of noise filling the kettle and finding mugs and things. It gave me time to breathe again, deep and slow.

'Tell me about yourself,' she said at last, and I realised from her voice that she wasn't quite breathing steadily herself. So I began to tell her about Mum and Dad, and the box of baby clothes, and the ammonite.

As I was telling my story Clair opened the door to come in and her mother motioned to her to be quiet. I quite liked the idea of her being there. Before she came in the air was so tense that it felt as if there was a tunnel between her mother and me, and that there was no light either side of it, and no give in it. When Clair came through the door and moved to the sink and then to the table I felt the whole room opening out again, filling up with air and light. The tension was gone.

Clair picked up the ammonite. 'This is nice,' she said. 'It reminds me of a catherine wheel.'

'My mother gave it to me,' I said.

'Sammy's trying to trace the house where he was born,' her mother told her, and I thanked her in my head for not telling her about my embarrassing mistake. What if I'd said it all to Clair first? What if I'd said to her, 'Guess what. You're my sister.' What on earth would she have thought of me?

'It's an ammonite,' I told her.

'I know. We've done fossils at school. We went to Dorset, didn't we, Mum, looking for fossils? Never found any.'

'My mother put it in my cradle when I was born.'

'Did she? What a lovely present!'

'Well now, Sammy,' Clair's mother interrupted us. 'It's getting late …'

'I know,' I said. I stood up and shoved the Sammy note and the ammonite back in my pocket. 'I think I'll be going now.'

'That's not what I meant, really. I mean, do you have anywhere to go to?'

'I was thinking of going back to the YHA,' I said. 'It's quite cheap there.'

'It's miles!' said Clair.

'About eight,' I told her. 'It's nothing really.' I remembered then that the warden had told me it would be closed. Oh well. There was still the hedge.

'Would you like to stay here?' She was so nice, Clair's mother. She was really, really nice.

'If I could just have a bit of floor space …'

'And in exchange, I want you to phone your mum and dad and tell them you're here.'

There's usually a catch when grown-ups are nice to me.

'I can't do that,' I said. 'I just can't do it.'

We talked round and round in circles. Clair's mother was very keen to let my parents know exactly where I was in case they wanted to contact me. I didn't want them to know in case it upset them.

'I'd rather tell them properly,' I said. 'Not just over the phone. They'll want to know everything …'

She nodded. 'Well, I do understand that, Sammy. And you will tell them? They'll want to help you, when you're older. There are ways of tracing your natural parents. I'm sure there are agencies set up to do just that. You don't have to trail round like Sherlock Holmes to do it.'

'No,' I said. I felt small and stupid and miserable. I'd felt glorious when I'd set off from the YHA that morning, like a knight on a quest. Now I felt like a silly little kid who couldn't sort his own head out.

'Why not just phone your coach in London? You don't have to explain anything to him, just give him our number,' Clair suggested.

'He'd be really mad with me,' I said. I could just imagine him saying down the phone 'If you don't need me, then I don't need you, my lad. I've got loads of kids waiting to take your place.'

What Clair's mum didn't do was to say 'You should

have thought about all this earlier,' or anything like that. She was clever. She just sat there watching me quietly and letting me think that out for myself.

'I just get these ideas in my head,' I said helplessly. 'When I really, really want to do something it just burns me till I do it.'

'And he has already talked to his mum and dad tonight,' Clair put in. She was on my side, every inch of the way. She just seemed to understand everything without having to have it explained to her. 'They do know he's alive.'

In the end her mother agreed that I could stay the night as long as I promised to go on to London the next day. She herself would take me to the station and put me on the train.

I did promise. I'd had enough. I knew I had no hope of finding my mother, not that way. She was right. Mum and Dad would know how to do it. They wouldn't stop me. I thought I'd been clever, but I'd been stupid. That was the last thing I thought about as I curled up in my sleeping bag on their settee, with the real fire settling down to ashes in the grate.

But by next morning, everything had changed.

Notes for Chapter 14

James believes he has found his goal. He asks to see Clair's grandmother. She remembers the name Sammy, but James finds that yet again he has not yet finished his search.

What do you think?
The author shows how Clair and her grandmother react to James. Think about:
- the way in which Clair and James get on with each other
- the way that Mrs Champion treats James, and how it is different from the way Clair's mother treats him.

Questions
In his excitement, James has made a number of assumptions which turn out to be mistaken.
1. What two mistakes has he made about Clair?
2. What mistakes has he made about Mrs Champion?
3. What does James find out about Mrs Champion which disappoints him?

Further activity
The author describes Mrs Champion in some detail. Write a pen-portrait of an older person whom you know well. You may have a grandparent or you may prefer to describe another relative or friend. Try to use language imaginatively to make your description more vivid. Remember that a portrait should include more than a description of the person's appearance. You need to convey their personality as well, perhaps by including some anecdotes about things they have done.

Chapter 14

It happened after we'd had breakfast, and Clair and I were washing up. Her mother went upstairs with a tray of breakfast for the grandmother. We were to leave immediately afterwards for the station.

'I wish I was coming with you,' Clair said. 'I get really bored here. There's nothing, absolutely nothing, to do.'

'I wish you were coming too,' I said. The thought of sharing a long train journey with her pleased me a lot. I really liked her. I would have liked her for a sister.

'Will you write to me?' she asked.

'Okay,' I said. 'You need to be good at translating, though.'

I wrote down my address for her as neatly as I could, but actually my hand was shaking a bit. I hoped she wouldn't notice. She started to write her own down.

'I'm not likely to forget where you live,' I reminded her.

She looked up, surprised. 'But I don't live here,' she said. 'It would drive me round the bend, living in a little village like this. Mum's come here because Gran's ill and I came for half-term to keep her company. We live in London.'

'So what's your Gran called?'

'Mrs Ellie Champion. It's a good name, that. I wish I was called Champion.'

'So do I,' I said gloomily. 'Diving Champion.'

'Sammy the champion!' Clair laughed.

But you see, it had started all over again, that ticking in my head. It was the last clue on the Sammy note. The first name. Not 'm' at all. 'on'. Champion. This time I kept it to myself, just nursing the thought in my head. Clair's mother must have seen it when she read the note, but she hadn't said anything. Surely her surname had been Champion before she married Clair's father.

'Can I see your gran?' I asked. It was a last clue to follow before I left. When I'd spoken to her I could truthfully tell myself that I'd done everything that could be done.

By this time Clair's mother was out in the garden, fetching some post from the green box down by the gate. Clair took me upstairs. I was desperate to meet her grandmother, but I was dreading having to talk to a sick old lady in bed. I was relieved to see that she was up and dressed and sitting by the window, and not very old at all.

'I'm watching the birds,' she said without turning her head round. 'I've got a pair of bluetits nesting in the tree-box and I'm expecting the chicks to start flying any day now. I'm not going to miss them just because Clair's brought her boyfriend in to see me, if you don't mind.'

'Gran! He's not …!'

Her gran laughed and Clair retreated, too embarrassed even to look at me. I didn't mind. It was an easy mistake to make. I walked straight up to Mrs Champion and sat down in the chair next to her. She had a kind, pale face and hair that had gone faded instead of white or grey. She looked very like Clair's mother. In a strange way she even looked like Clair. Her eyes were a kind of milky blue. She looked sideways at me and then gazed at the tree outside again.

'You've got a wonderful head of hair, young man.'

I was used to people saying that to me, particularly people's grandmothers. I never know what you're supposed to say in reply. Sometimes I mutter, 'No, I haven't.' Or, 'Thank you. So have you.' Or sometimes, 'Actually it all fell out when I was three and this is a wig,' depending on who I'm talking to. Usually I just ignored it and pretended I hadn't heard. But this time I thought it was an important clue. So I came straight out with it.

'I'm Sammy.'

She twisted herself round in her chair to look at me properly. 'Sammy, Sammy, Sammy,' she murmured, kind of chanting it to herself, as if she was reaching into her memory for something. She let out a long, slow sigh and leaned back, shaking her head slightly. 'Are you adopted, Sammy?'

'Yes,' I said.

She did know who I was. It was obvious by her face, by the puzzled, astonished way she was looking at me, by the way her hand fluttered out as if to touch my hair. I ducked my head down. I didn't know what to think now.

'My little Sammy. After all this time.'

So Ellie Champion was the one. Not really old at all, not like Grandma Logan. But old all the same, with faded hair and milky eyes. This wasn't what I'd dreamed about at all. How could she be my mother?

'Poor little Sammy. Do you know, I was only thinking about you the other day. I always think about you when it's coming up to Clair's birthday. I think, what's he doing now? Where is he? Is he well? And most of all, I think – what does he look like? If only I could see him. That's what I say to myself, time and time again.'

I felt awkward. I didn't know what to do with myself, the way she was gazing at me, shaking her head and smiling. I hadn't wanted her to be like this, old and ill. I didn't know what to say.

'Are you happy, Sammy, with your adoptive parents?'

'Yes,' I said quickly. I thought fleetingly of Mum, with her busy, bright ways, and of big, laughing, noisy Dad, his bad jokes. I felt guilty and suddenly homesick for them. I wondered whether I'd ever be able to tell them how I'd spent the last few days.

'They must love you very much,' she said. 'When people want a child so much that they're willing to bring up someone else's as their own it means they've got a lot of love to give. How much they wanted you! You're a lucky boy.'

'I know,' I said. My lips were dry and sticking together. I stood up, wanting to leave then. I didn't think I had anything left to say to her.

'And your little mother, too,' she went on.

I stopped by the door. My heart was doing slow cartwheels in my chest.

'I think she must have loved you, too, in her way. I suppose that's what you've come for, is it Sammy? To find out about her? All I can tell you, love, is how I found you. Will that help?'

Notes for Chapter 15

Ellie Champion tells James how she found him, and how she later decided to give him up for adoption. She tells James where she thinks his birth mother had come from. James decides that he cannot return to his parents without completing his search. He borrows a tent and sets off up the hill.

What do you think?
During Mrs Champion's story, James learns a great deal about people's feelings. As you read the chapter, think about:
- why Ellie Champion felt that finding the baby was a miracle
- how James felt as he heard her story
- how Clair showed her understanding of James' feelings
- how Clair's mother's attitude to James has changed.

Questions
In this chapter the author describes how James has to cope with a great deal of new information about himself and others. Look for places in the text which will help you to answer these questions.

1. What does Ellie Champion tell James about his birth mother?

2. How does Ellie Champion show that both his birth mother and his adoptive parents must have loved him?

3. What conclusions does James come to about girls when he compares his birth mother with Clair and girls he has known at school?

4. Why did Ellie Champion keep secret the possible identity of James' birth mother?

5. How do Ellie Champion's expectations of James differ from those of her daughter Frances (Clair's mother)?

Further activity
Writers like to end chapters of a story with what they call a 'hook'. This is rather like the baited lure a fisherman uses, and is intended to 'catch' you and make you want to read on. Look through the story so far and see how many chapters end with a short sentence which leads you on to the next chapter. Copy some of these sentences down. Say which chapter each comes from, and after each one write down your ideas of why they are effective in making you want to read on.

Chapter 15

'It was a bitterly cold morning in late February,' Ellie Champion began. 'The day before had been blue and sunny and looked like the beginning of spring, even though the tops of the mountains still had a covering of snow. But when I looked out of the window on that particular day the sky was grey and there was a blizzard of sleet. Soon it will snow again, I thought, and all those crocuses and daffodils that are beginning to poke through had better shut up shop and tuck themselves back into the soil again, nice and warm. They never do, though, do they? Funny how they keep going.

'This was about fifteen years ago, by the way. It was about a year after my husband had died. Frances was living abroad with her husband, and she was expecting Clair. I used to watch out every day for a letter from her. As I was looking out of this very window I saw a girl coming down the track. She had a dog with her. And she seemed to be carrying something in her arms. I didn't take much notice at the time. I do remember thinking that she wasn't dressed like a hiker, but she did have a nice warm coat on. Black, it was. And I thought no more about her. I was worrying about the birds. I came down and just went down my path a bit to scatter a few pieces of bread crusts and seeds, and then I scuttled back in out of the cold.

'It must have been an hour or so before I went out again. I'd decided to stay in that day, because I had plenty to do in the house without getting myself battered and stung with that blizzard. But then I remembered that I hadn't looked for my post. When I went outside, the sleet had turned to snow. It was perfectly lovely. The wind had dropped, and these big, soft flakes were falling, and it was very peaceful. I went down to the post-box and opened it up – and there, I had the biggest shock and surprise of my life! There inside it, muffled up in a sack, was a newborn baby! I couldn't even tell whether it was dead or alive.

'I picked up the little thing and rocked it next to my heart. I hurried into the house with it and cuddled it by the fire. It was alive!' Her voice filled up then, and she had to stop for a bit. 'Sammy, Sammy, you were alive!'

Right until she got to that part I didn't realise she was telling me something about myself. I remember giving a little kind of gasp then, and she put her hand on mine as if she thought I was crying.

'I wrapped you round with warm towels from the airing-cupboard and you started whimpering. I found a piece of paper in the sacking, where she'd scribbled a note on the back of an envelope she'd torn open.

"Look after Sammy." And a stone, a bit of a keepsake.'

I took them out of my pocket and she took them from me, nodding. She cradled the ammonite in her hand.

'I thought of that girl coming over the Tor there and I knew it was her. What could have driven her to do a thing like that? Panic, I thought. Terror, maybe, in case her parents found out. My heart went out to her. Whatever happens, I thought, I'll keep her secret. The child will be all right now. That's what matters. Maybe I was wrong.

Maybe we should all be made to face up to the consequences of our actions. But at the time, that's what I decided to do.

'This is the important thing, Sammy, and you must never, never forget this. That girl did what she did because she loved you. She could have left you up there on the mountain and no one would ever have known. But she didn't. It took a lot of courage to do what she did for you. She risked her life to do it. But she saved yours.'

Clair's mother came in and sat by us. She stroked Ellie's hand and took the ammonite from it. 'Have you been telling Sammy his story, Mum?'

So she had known all the time.

'I have. And he's a brave boy. It's not what he wanted to hear about his mother.'

She was right. I was shocked and bewildered. In all my daydreams, this kind of thing had never occurred to me. When Clair came smiling into the room with a tray of coffee for us all I could hardly bear to look at her. So my mother could have been as young as she was when she had me. She was a girl who was into pop music, perhaps, going out dancing, scribbling pop stars' names on the back of school exercise books, giggling about older boys at school. A girl from our class had a baby last term and we all called her 'the slag'. Was that what they'd have called my mother? No wonder my parents hadn't wanted to tell me about her. At least they were saving me from this kind of shame.

'Where will your journey end, Sammy?' Ellie Champion's voice came suddenly out of the jangle of cups and spoons on the tray. I realised that Clair and her mother were gathering them in again; coffee had been drunk, shopping-lists written, and all that time I'd been sitting hunched in my chair with my head right down. Her voice hauled me up from somewhere under deep water.

'My journey?'

Clair and her mother went quietly out of the room, closing the door behind them.

'Your search for your mother? The adoption society won't be able to tell you anything. They don't know as much as I do. Is there anything more you want me to tell you now?'

I kept thinking about my tiny little self abandoned in a piece of sacking. I could have died. 'Was I very ill when you found me?'

'Very weak. Very hungry, though you'd be surprised how long babies can survive before they have their first feed. I sent for the local midwife straight away, of course – she only lived a few doors away. She came round with a bottle and baby milk and she let me give it to you. Oh, my heart went out to you then, Sammy! Have you seen a tiny baby feeding? They know how to suck from that very first moment! It's wonderful to see. A bottle's not as good as the real thing, but I had none of that, of course.'

I shifted uneasily in my chair.

'Anyway, I was stocked up with baby clothes, as it

happened. Frances was expecting Clair at the time, as I said, and like any good grandmother I'd been knitting away for months! I had a little blue outfit that was just right. Well, it was enormous on you, but it was the right colour! I rang the police next and they scoured the village for your mother. I kept the secret. In the end they assumed that you'd been brought by car and dumped here. I don't think it ever occurred to them, on that snowy day, that a little mite of a thing could have plodded over the mountain with you, on a track that only the sheep come down! You were a miracle, Sammy!

'I wanted to keep you, very much. I would have loved to keep you. But I knew I couldn't give a baby a proper home, not at my age – just as that child over the mountains knew that she couldn't. I fostered you for a couple of weeks and then the adoption society handed you over to the people who were over the moon with happiness at the thought of having you. Your mum and dad. I dressed you in your little blue outfit and put you in a crib with your note and your stone, and I thought I'd never see you again. I really did. Thank you for coming back, Sammy.'

'It's all right,' I said, vague. My head was hurting so much that I wasn't sure what I was saying actually.

'That's the track she came down. Can you see it?'

She pointed out a twisty, windy path that seemed to disappear up the mountainside.

'That's Horsenose Tor, up there. See how it flattens out at the top like a horse's head. That's why this cottage has such an odd name. And your mother lived over there somewhere.'

I said goodbye to her and somehow I got myself downstairs. My head was spinning. I couldn't think clearly. I couldn't even see clearly. I heard Clair and her mother talking outside and I just went out and stood by them. I was helpless. I couldn't connect with anything.

'Time we were setting off for the station,' Clair's mother said. 'Did you find out what you wanted to know?'

'Sort of,' I said. 'Not really.'

Clair and I stood by the gate while her mother backed the car out of the garage. I saw the post-box on the wall, the green paint blistered and peeling. It was like a bird-box. I lifted up the lid. It was just big enough for a new-born baby to fit in. I closed the lid and stood looking up at Horsenose Tor. Its long ridge was shrouded in mist.

Somewhere over the other side of it was the house where I was born.

Don't remember walking back over the Tor.

All I remember is someone putting warm arms round me and whispering into my face to make me open my eyes.

I was lying by our gate. Caroline was crouching over me.

Heard the crows. Heard Bob whimpering, and the sheep in the fields bleating.

Caroline took my hands. Led me into the kitchen. Michael was doing the fire. When he saw me he dropped the sticks and ran out, 'Father, Father, she's here! Our Elizabeth's back home!'

122

There was Father with his boots still on, glaring in the doorway, mad with me.

'Father, leave her! Can't you see she's ill!'

I want to sleep. I just want to sleep.

That was my voice, whimpering like a child's. Cold, cold, and hurting deep inside.

Tried to go upstairs, and Caroline caught hold of me.

Father's voice echoing round me, asking me questions.

Just want to sleep, right here on the rug by the fire. Let me sleep.

'I know where she's been.' That was Caroline, soft and kind, her hair brushing my face as she bent over me, lifting me and stroking me.

'She's been with Mam. Don't hurt her. She's been with Mam all night.'

'Ready?' Clair's mother called. She opened the boot of the car, then, when I didn't move, got out and came over to me to pick up my sportsbag.

'I don't think he is, Mum.' Clair's voice came from somewhere far away. I came hurtling back to my senses. I told them both what Ellie Champion had told me.

'I can't do it,' I said helplessly. 'I can't just get in the car and then the train and go all the way to London …'

'… without seeing what's on the other side of Horsenose Tor.' Clair finished the sentence for me, following with her eyes the track that I was staring at.

Clair's mother sighed and put down the sportsbag.

'My journey isn't over.' I was quoting Ellie Champion

but it all sounded a bit wild and romantic coming from me.

'He's come all this way, Mum,' Clair pleaded. 'On his own. He can't just go away now and give up.'

'Isn't your diving more important at the moment, Sammy?' her mother said. 'You've got a big competition at the weekend. Horsenose Tor isn't going to go away overnight. You could come back any time. With your mum and dad. Wouldn't that be the way to do it?'

But it wasn't the way I wanted to do it. She could see that, really. I was yearning to do it now, my way. I wanted to make the journey that my mother had made fifteen years ago, along the sheep-track, right over the top of the Tor.

The thing about me is, when I really want something I just won't be budged. I suppose that's what makes me into the sort of person who can spend three hours a night jumping off a concrete slab to get one dive right.

Clair's mother put the car away and we went back into the house. She wanted me to have lunch first. I was so brimming with excitement that I could hardly eat, but I did as I was told. I was getting my own way, after all.

'I'm ashamed to say that I've never been over there myself,' she confessed. 'I've been up to the top with my husband and we've walked along the ridge, but I've never gone down the other side. Mind you, we could drive you round. It's probably about twenty miles round by road but there must be a way into the valley from the other end …'

I shook my head. If my mother had walked over that track, then that was the way I wanted to go. There was no point otherwise.

'It's a long walk, Sammy, and pretty strenuous. I doubt if you'll get there and back before night-time. Not if you want to explore the valley properly. If you must go, why not stay the night and start really early tomorrow?'

But that wouldn't do. My heart was set on going immediately. It was Clair who solved the problem. She went rummaging in the cupboard under the stairs and came back with a small rolled-up tent.

'It won't do you much good if it rains heavily, but Tommy and I used to camp in Gran's garden with it.'

'Who's Tommy?' I asked, surprising myself with a sudden flare of jealousy. Clair blushed.

'My brother, of course.'

It was amazing how she understood everything I was thinking.

Her mother stuffed fruit cake and apples and sandwiches into my bag. I couldn't have done any of this without them. If I'd waited till I was older I could have done it all without anyone's help. But sometimes things burn inside you so fiercely that nothing will put them out.

'Now,' she said, when my bag was full and waiting by the door. 'There's one more thing to do before you go. You phone your parents.' She stood there, immovable, her arms folded, with that set look on her face that grown-ups have when they know they're in the right and they won't take any argument from you. 'I don't mind what you tell them, Sammy. That's your business. But I absolutely insist that you let them know where in the world you are and who they can contact if they need to get hold of you. All right?'

Clair glanced at me in sympathy and she and her mother both left the room so I could make the call in private. It was the last thing in the world I wanted to do. I rang the hotel and was told they were out.

'Please tell them I rang to say hello,' I asked the receptionist. 'And everything's fine.' I put the receiver down and tapped it with my fingers, not knowing what to do next. 'I couldn't think of the right message to leave them,' I said to the door, knowing that Clair's mother would be on the other side of it, pretending to be busy dusting or something.

'The man in London,' she called back.

'Mum …!' I heard Clair protesting.

I dreaded making that call even more than phoning Mum and Dad. I dutifully rang the number, with my heart somewhere round my ankles, hoping against hope that Ken would be out. He wasn't.

'Where the hell are you?' he shouted as soon as he heard my voice. 'You're supposed to be training with me!'

'I'm sorry Ken, I …'

'And don't try to kid me that you're with Matt because I know you're not. I rang his father last night.'

'I'm staying with some friends,' I said. 'It's very important, Ken.'

'So's your diving important – or it is to me. It was to me.

Used to be. Not any more, Sonny Jim. People only let me down once. I can't go wasting my time like this on kids like you who couldn't give a damn. There's plenty more where you came from. Kids who'll be glad of the chance.'

I had to hold the phone away from my ear. I knew how hurt he was. I understood why he was angry. I thought of his letter to me. It used to be my most precious thing. When I could manage to make him listen I gave him the phone number of Horsenose Cottage and then put down the receiver. There was no point trying to say anything else. He didn't want to hear it.

So I was very subdued when I set off with my sportsbag full of tent and apples and sandwiches later that afternoon. Clair came with me for the first half hour or so. She couldn't get a word out of me. I think she was quite relieved when we reached the waterfall where she'd promised her mother she'd turn back. It was a steep pull up there, and we were hot and thirsty by the time we reached it. Clair cupped water in her hands and drank it, and I stuck my head right in the water. It was amazingly cold and clear. It took my breath away. Clair laughed and I turned to look at her. Her hair was damp and sticking to her face and for a second I thought of Jan from our class, and the way she'd looked that night at the fair. I knew that I liked Clair much more.

I told you she understood me. She got right inside my head and knew me. It was uncanny. Because what she did then, when I was looking at her and thinking a lot and saying nothing, was this. She put her arms on my shoulders and hugged me. It was just a quick, shy hug. It made me go dizzy. She pushed her hair away from her face and turned away, as shy as I was.

'See you tomorrow, Sammy. Good luck!'

And then she was gone, scrambling down the path as if she was being followed by a herd of cows. She didn't turn round once, but I watched until the track twisted away from me and she was out of sight. I couldn't believe that I'd known her for less than twenty-four hours.

And then I turned back and looked at the way the track snaked up and up the steep slope. I was on my own then. Really alone.

I've never climbed a mountain before. I'm not sure when a hill is a mountain but it seemed pretty high to me. I kept getting out of breath and had to keep stopping to look back. When I was really high up I just caught a glimpse of Ellie Champion's cottage, and behind it the whole of Hollygate and Nether Hollygate spilled out. I could see where the road looped back and would eventually meet the lane that came down from the Youth Hostel. Somewhere between them must be the waterfall tree. I felt as if I had entered a new life since I had first set out. Here I was Sammy.

I wondered what Clair was doing, and whether she was thinking about me at all. She might be helping her mother to get the tea ready, or sitting in Ellie Champion's room pretending to talk to her, looking out at the track and trying to spot me. That's what I hoped she'd be doing. I waved, and felt silly. What if she was watching me through a pair of binoculars? I pretended I was swotting flies away and then, because I felt even sillier, I put down my sportsbag and did a backwards somersault. A mountaineering sheep skittered away from me in fright. I felt great.

The sky seemed to be full of the song of a bird that I couldn't even see, it was so high up. It seemed to be bursting with joy, filling every tiny fraction of space with its song. I couldn't hear anything except for the sound of that tiny bird. I felt like singing myself. I was feeling happy for the first time since that night at the fair. I knew I was doing the right thing. I picked up my bag and ran to the very summit of Horsenose Tor.

Notes for Chapter 16

James climbs to the summit of the tor and descends to the valley beyond. He sets up the tent but is evicted by the landowner and has to move to a campsite. In the morning, he finds that the weather has turned to rain.

What do you think?
As you read the chapter you will have found several references to things which affect James' mood. Notice how he reacts to:
- the birds and the scenery at the top of the hill
- the gloom of the next valley
- the attitude of the campsite owner
- the change in the weather.

Questions
You will find evidence in the chapter to help you with these questions:
1. What makes James feel that the valley he is entering is unfriendly?
2. How do James' plans for this part of his journey compare with his plans so far?
3. Find evidence that James' feelings about the valley are justified.
4. What is similar about Elizabeth's mother's opinion of gypsies and the campsite owner's attitude to James? Find words that describe this sort of attitude.

Further activity
There are several words and phrases in this chapter which use exaggeration to get the effect the author wants. Often when we are describing particularly enjoyable or unpleasant memories we use expressions which would not normally be used in this way. Read again the paragraph where James describes his difficulties in erecting his tent and the way the midges attack him. Make a list of some of these phrases and write their real meaning beside them. (For example, James says that erecting his tent took a million years, which is a more colourful way of saying that it took him rather a long time and that he was in a hurry.)

Look back at some recent examples of your own writing to see if you ever use this technique, or where you might have used it to good effect.

Chapter 16

Only it wasn't the summit. Every time I thought I'd reached the top it rolled up away from me. The song of the tiny bird faded away. The track was cluttered with boulders, I kept tripping and losing my balance. Big, clumsy, brown birds kept rising up from the ground right in front of me, frightening the life out of me with their suddenness and their loud voices. Apart from them it was eerie. I've never known such quiet.

By the time I reached the real top I was almost too tired to walk. I've never felt so completely alone in my life. I was too high up even for the sheep. I couldn't hear anything, but the silence was like a weight inside me. I wanted to run back down to Clair's house. I stood at the top of the Tor with the day beginning to grow grey and cold around me, willing myself to go on. I couldn't stay up there all night, that was for sure, not in all that wilderness of rocks. I closed my eyes and thought of the safe, familiar streets of home, the orange street lamps and the glow of house lights and the flickering of television screens in every room; the neat gardens, the steady hum of cars.

From where I was standing I could see both valleys. Clair's was still sunny. Mine was in shadow. It looked gloomy and cold down there. Before I reached the bottom I'd be walking into darkness. It was like a hidden valley, a secret.

All the time I was walking I was trying to imagine what

it must have been like for my real mother coming up from the other side in the cold and the dark. I wondered whether she'd been scared. I wondered why she'd had to do it.

Well, that was what I'd come for. There really wasn't any going back now. So I set off down into the secret valley, and that was the second big achievement of my life.

I knew the baby would always have to be a secret.

The summer before Mam died I knew that the wild boy had to be a secret.

We met often and we laughed together. He called me his queen and said he'd take me riding out of the valley. I kept all that secret.

But Caroline told on me to Mam.

'Our Elizabeth talks to one of the wild boys in Uncle Staff's field.' Bright as anything, just for nothing she told her.

I pulled faces at her while Mam wasn't looking. None of Caroline's business. My secret.

'She does. I seen her.'

Mam's face went snappy and hard. 'No, you don't, Elizabeth Frith. Oh no, you don't.'

'I do, Mam,' I laughed. 'He's nice.'

'He's not nice,' Mam said, and she was banging the pots on the table like drums. She scared me a bit, she did then. She made Michael cry, and Peter woke up in his cot. 'They're wicked, Elizabeth. And anyone who talks to them is wicked, too'.

'Wicked, wicked, wicked.' Michael copied her like it was a song to sing, banging with his hands. He was still crying a bit, though. Mam lifted him up over her big baby-belly and kissed him. She loved her babies, Mam did.

The path down into the secret valley was very steep and stony – in fact it seemed to be the bed of a dried-up stream. I had to sling my sportsbag across my back and stick both my arms through the handles so I had both hands free. Then I had to clamber down backwards, clinging at the heather and the twisty little thorny trees at the side of the track while my feet skidded and slid away from me. I was scared stiff in case I lost my grip and went hurtling down the valley-side in an avalanche of boulders. 'Go back! Go Back! Go back!' the birds kept cackling at me, and I would have done, too, only the thought of going back again was even worse than the thought of carrying on down.

When I could trust myself to turn round and stand up properly I could see the path I should have been on, snaking away to the left of me. But I was more than half-way down the valley-side. I carried on along my dried-up stream and it met up with a proper stream with a grassy bank between them. I drank some of the water, remembering Clair at the other side of the Tor drinking from the waterfall. I missed her already. How could I miss her when I'd only just met her? I went through a list of all the people at school who I quite liked and realised I didn't miss any of them.

I ate some of my food and then decided it would be a good place to put up the tent. I'd no idea what time it was because I'd left my watch in the bathroom at Clair's house, along with my contact lenses. I'd bent one of the arms of my glasses when I was coming down that stream bed. When I tried to straighten it I snapped it off completely. I didn't even have a sticking plaster to mend it with. I hooked the good arm over my ear and they sort of worked. At least I could see, in a lop-sided sort of way, though if I looked down the glasses slid off my nose. But it could have been worse. Clair could have been there to see me making a spectacle of myself, as Dad would have said.

Anyway, I'd had enough scrambling about for the day. I was tired out. Now that I'd eaten I even began to feel quite cheerful. It would be something to tell the Griffin about, this would. Camping by a stream out in the wilds. It was probably the sort of thing he did every weekend.

I unrolled the tent and took a million years trying to work out how to put it up. The midges were coming out and started attacking me as if they'd suddenly discovered a jam sandwich, swarming at me in armies, biting chunks out of me and spitting me out so I could see my blood oozing. In the end I gave up trying to flap them away and crawled into the tent, zipped it up, and hid inside the sleeping bag.

It was strange to be lying there in a tent in the middle of nowhere with the sky still light. All around me sheep were bleating away to each other as if they were out carol-singing and couldn't remember the tunes. But I was very tired, glad to be stretched out. My feet were throbbing and my head was aching, too. I kept going over the things that Ellie Champion had said. They didn't make sense any more. This morning when I was sitting in her sunny room listening to the story and gazing up at Horsenose Tor it had seemed like a romantic sort of quest, to climb over the very top into the other valley. It was like something out of the tales of King Arthur. But it wasn't like that any more. I couldn't picture that young girl with her bundle of sacking and her dog. I didn't believe she could have done what I'd just done, in the winter as well, and just after I'd been born. I didn't believe any of it, or that it could have had anything to do with me.

Yet I had the ammonite. That was the token of my birth. That was real enough. I pulled it out of my pocket, where it was digging into my thigh, and lay with it cupped between my hands under my chin. I was in a turmoil about everything and I was feeling lonely. I wanted Mum. She would have made me a hot drink and found me something to soothe the midge bites.

I wanted Clair, too. I wanted to talk to her and have a laugh. I wish she didn't live so far away. London! If only there were girls like Clair at my school. If only Clair was there. I must have drifted away on that thought because when I heard someone unzipping my tent I thought for a crazy moment that it was Clair. A woman was talking to me in a hissing, angry voice that didn't belong in my dream. I pulled my senses together and realised that she was asking me what on earth I thought I was doing. She pulled my tent flap wide open and peered in at me. A sheepdog squeezed past her and started digging inside my sleeping bag as if he thought there was a sheep in there.

'Please don't let them in,' I begged.

'Who? Are there more of you?'

'The midges. I'm trying to keep away from them.'

The woman whistled between her teeth and the dog crept out on its belly, obviously disappointed that she wouldn't let him have a go at me.

'It looks to me as if you were trying to camp here,' she said. 'Were you?'

Before I could even answer she'd started pulling up the pegs. The tent sagged miserably around me and the midges clamoured in.

'It's not allowed. There's a camping field down there next to the farm, with proper facilities. That's where you go.'

'I didn't know,' I said.

'We can't have people sticking tents up just like this, wherever they fancy. Would your parents want people to go sticking tents up in their garden? This is a working place, not a holiday home ...'

On and on she went while I was scrambling out of my sleeping bag and rolling up the tent. The dog tried to be rolled up with it. She didn't call him off, just stood and watched while he got in the way and I kept dropping things. She still stood there, arms on her hips, while I staggered off, and I'd only gone down the track a few yards when I thought about my ammonite. I remembered I'd been holding it before I dropped off to sleep and I didn't remember packing it again. It wasn't in my pockets. I thought about going back for it the next morning but I knew I'd never find it then. So I had to turn round and go back to her.

'What now?' she demanded. 'Need a compass to go downhill?'

'I've dropped something,' I said.

It was nearly dark. I groped round on my hands and knees, turning pebbles over and sifting through them with the dog sniffing round my fingers. My glasses kept sliding off. The woman crouched down, interested.

'What is it you've lost? Money? Your watch?'

I didn't answer her. I was desperate to find it.

'What does it look like?'

There it was, at last. I scooped it up and she held out her hand to look at it. I pushed it into my pocket.

'A stone,' she said. 'I see. Well, at least we can go, now you've found your stone.'

She followed me all the way down to the farm. My bag was banging against my shins because I couldn't be bothered to carry it properly. I suppose I wanted her to realise how tired I was. Bats were flinging themselves round my head like flying missiles. I would have given anything to be back home.

The woman stopped as we came to a gate leading to the farm buildings and pointed to a field at the side of it. A few tents were pitched there, glowing with torches or little Gazlights. I could hear a low murmuring of voices. Maybe it wouldn't be as lonely here as it was up on the hillside, I thought.

'Toilets and wash-room over behind the trees. I'll take your money in the morning.'

And she was gone before I could ask her how much it might be. I didn't even know if I could afford it.

'So you don't go there again,' Caroline told me.

But I did. The wild boy made me happy. Said I was his queen. Said we'd live in his caravan and go with the wild people.

'Go where?' I asked him. 'Manchester?'

'Everywhere, queen. All kinds of places like you've never even dreamed about. Horse fairs. You'd like them. We'd go through big cities, and villages, and down to the sea, and sometimes over the sea. Everywhere, we'd go.'

'And not never come back home?' How could I breathe if I didn't have the mountains around me, and the fields and the moors? 'I'd die.'

'Come here, queen. Would I let you die?'

I woke up to the sound of rain. When I looked out of the tent the hills had disappeared into a mist. I crawled back into my sleeping bag and ate some more of the food that Clair's mother had given me. Then I realised that the rain was seeping through the tent. I rolled everything up, which was an awful job in the rain. The tent was twice as bulky as it had been before and wouldn't go back into its bag, however much I punched it and squeezed it. I'd wanted to sneak away before the farmer woman came round for the money but I was too late. She came squelching across the field in her wellies and with the dog joyfully hurling itself at crows behind her. She spoke to him once and he slunk over to her and crouched behind her. It must be fantastic to have that kind of power.

She was slightly less aggressive once I'd paid up.

'Are you having a little holiday here?' she asked me.

It was the last place on earth I'd want to come to for a holiday. The farmyard smelt worse than the lavatories at school and her campsite was like the playing field after a football match in January.

'No,' I said. 'I just wanted to see it, but I'm going home now. I haven't any money left, anyway.'

I was hoping she might let me off my camping fee. After all, I'd only been there a few hours.

'Don't go without looking round the village,' she said. 'We're very proud of our little church.'

I don't know why grown-ups think churches and things are interesting. They all do. Every holiday I've been on Mum and Dad have dragged me round a church to look at the windows and everything. They're all exactly the same, as far as I can tell. And they're cold.

'Have you got your stone this time?' she called after me.

She was actually laughing.

I trudged off. My blisters were burning my heels.

Behind the mossy stone walls sheep bleated miserably. Some of them had terrible coughs. It didn't surprise me, the way they have to stand about in damp fields all day. I couldn't imagine how anyone could live in a place like this.

Notes for Chapters 17 and 18

Elizabeth's story has been becoming increasingly agitated as she remembers her wild boy and what happened when her parents found out what she had been doing with him. James continues his journey down the valley. He finds the atmosphere unfriendly in comparison with the town life he is accustomed to.

What do you think?
In these chapters we see that Elizabeth is aware that what she has done will upset her parents. She feels guilty but continues to see the wild boy. James also feels guilty about lying to his parents. As you read, think about:
- how Elizabeth and James make excuses for behaviour which they know is wrong
- whether they feel they are being punished for it
- how the author uses situations and words to make you sympathetic towards both of them.

Questions
1. How does the author make us feel that James is not in complete control of his actions?
2. Why does Elizabeth's mother realise what has happened between Elizabeth and the wild boy?
3. Why does the author say that James feels that he has made no impression on his birthplace?
4. What reasons can you find in the text for the unfriendliness between the wild people and the inhabitants of the valley?

Further activity
People in the valley must have been aware both of the arrival and the sudden departure of the gypsies. Imagine that you work on the local newspaper. Write a series of brief articles reporting these events. Give your articles suitable date lines to show you have understood the time scale of the story. You could make up comments from local inhabitants to include in your articles. Look at a copy of your local paper to see how such articles are set out and the sort of language used. You could use a suitable computer program to present your work like a real newspaper.

Chapter 17

I know it was wicked. I know Father would have beaten me for the things that I did with the wild boy.

'You're my queen,' the wild boy said. 'We're married now.'

Married was being in church. I knew that. I knew I wasn't really his queen. In a place in my head I knew I'd never go riding out of the valley with him. That's how I knew it was wicked, what we did.

And the other way I knew it was wicked was because of what happened to Mam.

But I couldn't leave it, you see. The thing that had drawn me there was keeping me there. It was as if I was under some kind of spell, but that's daft talk, I know. I had this sort of pact with myself. 'Look at every house here,' I told myself. 'Go up every lane and track. Don't leave anything out. Then, when you've seen everything there is to see, you can go home and never come back.'

'Are we really married?' I asked him.

'We're as married as my mother and father are,' he said. 'She was fourteen, and he was sixteen, and they got married same way as us, no different, Elizabeth.'

Mam was married at sixteen. But she had a shiny golden ring on her finger to show for it.

'Give us a ring then,' I laughed. 'Like Mam's.'

'What you want a ring for? You wouldn't wear it.'

'To look at,' I told him. 'So's I'd know.'

Next time he saw me he gave me a stone. I'd never seen such a queer thing before. It was all curled up like a little snake. I liked it, though.

'What is it?' I asked him. 'Not a snail, is it?'

'It's a snake-stone. It's my best thing, that. It's millions of years' old.'

'Go on!' I said. 'That old!'

'You have it, Elizabeth. Now you know we're married, don't you?'

It was a very long valley. Miles and miles. I found a post office and bought a hot drink there. I still had quite a lot of food left over from the stuff Clair's mum had given me. I rang my parents' hotel again and just left a message at the switchboard to say I was having a great time. As I said, it wasn't often I told lies but when I did they were whoppers. Then I set off on the long, damp trudge. It never stopped drizzling all day. There was hardly anyone about, just a few farmers on tractors and the occasional cyclist, and millions of damp sheep. I wondered how far it was to the nearest swimming pool, or cinema.

What on earth did people do to enjoy themselves? It was a mystery.

'Elizabeth. Why are you smiling?' Caroline asked me.

'Secret,' I said, smiling still more.

We were in the pantry, whispering. She pulled my hair so I showed her my secret.

'An old stone!' she crowed. 'Mooning over a bit of stone!'

'It's a dead snake.'

'It never is.'

'It's a million years' old, Caroline.'

'Mam!' Caroline shouted. 'That wild boy's given Elizabeth a present!'

Mam looked at me then, and she knew everything. Mam always was like that.

The snake-stone was nothing. She wouldn't even look at it. But a present from the wild boy told her all my secrets, my queen and my kingdom, my kisses and my lovings, my marriage to him.

She shook me till we were all crying, her as well. She couldn't stop, in her ragings.

Caroline ran for Father, and he went shouting round to Uncle Staff's next door.

When they came back Uncle Staff had his shotgun with him. My father went to get his; the one he uses for shooting rabbits. They were grim, both of them. Mam stopped her hollering then.

'What are you thinking of doing?' she said, and there was quiet like winter cold all around her.

We all stopped our sobbing. Caroline held Peter in her arms. We were as silent as death with fearing.

'Driving them out, that's what,' said Father.

By the end of the day I was nearly back where I'd started from, and I felt pretty sure that I had seen everything there was to see. I had walked down every farm track, been barked at by about fifty-seven dogs, seen the front door of every cottage. I knew how the river curved and where the bridges were, and I was even beginning to recognise individual sheep. By the end of the day I could hardly stand up. I looked up at the track that led up Horsenose Tor and I knew I couldn't make it that night. Better to have a night's rest and set off first thing. I'd see Clair again.

I trudged back to the village shop. The woman who owned it hardly looked at me when I went in. There was another woman in the shop giving her some eggs from a basket, and they seemed set on having a good old gossip. I chose the bits of food I could afford and paid for them without them even stopping talking to each other. That was it, then. I'd seen the place where I'd been born, and I'd made no impression on it at all. I'd go away and it would be just as if I'd never been there, except perhaps for a few bent tufts of grass where my tent had been the night before, and a few muddy footprints down the lane.

I was starving by then. I needed somewhere sheltered to eat my food. I tried the church door, thinking that if there was a god in there, and I was never quite sure about whether there was or not, but if there was one he surely wouldn't mind if I ate my sandwiches in his church. Anyway, it was locked. I sat in the porch and ate them. The dampness of the air had got into my skin and bones, making me shiver, though it wasn't exactly cold. Rooks were cawing away up in the high, dark trees as if they were cross with the world. I felt as if they were saying to me, 'Go away. Go home. You don't belong here.'

Chapter 18

They went down to Uncle Staff's field, where the wild people had their vans. From our kitchen we could hear Uncle Staff shouting.

Then Mam grabbed my hand and started pulling me, dragging me away from the table where I was sitting with my snake-stone in my hands and my eyes shut tight.

'There'll be murder,' she said in the back of her throat. 'It'll be all your fault, Elizabeth.'

She dragged me down to the field. We could see the lights and the golden fires. We could see Uncle Staff and my father, crouched with their shot-guns by the trees. Father was ready to fire when Mam reached him. She ran yelling and pulled back his arm. His shot went wide, shimmeying up into the tree.

'Damn you!' he shouted. 'We're not shooting to kill them, Meg.'

And I've never heard such shouting and anger, such running and roaring and thudding of horsehooves, such terrible rumble of wheels.

All my life long it will roar in my head, the terrible, panicking stamping of horses.

By the end of the night it was over. The whole camp was gone. I never saw Sam, my wild boy. Never saw him again.

And before morning, Mam's baby started to come. It was too early. It was the wrong way round.

It killed my Mam.

That's what my wickedness did.

Notes for Chapters 19, 20 and 21

James makes a discovery which persuades him that he has found his goal. Elizabeth tries to come to terms with her mother's death and the loss of her baby. After many years of loneliness, she decides to marry one of the farm workers.

What do you think?
In these three chapters the author concentrates mainly on Elizabeth's story. As you read, think about:
- how the author has given us clues to the main characters in Elizabeth's story
- why Elizabeth decides to marry
- why the author focuses mainly on Elizabeth at this point.

Questions
1. How does the author make us feel that James is near the end of his quest?
2. How has Caroline's attitude to Elizabeth changed?
3. What sort of person is Joseph Rowlin?
4. What does Elizabeth do to help her decide to marry?
5. What does the future hold for Elizabeth when she marries?

Further activity
Use a dictionary to find out the meaning of the word 'simile'. Look in these three chapters for examples of similes. Take a sheet of paper and divide it into three columns. Head the first column *Simile*, the next column *Meaning* and the third column *Reasons*. Write in the first column the similes you have found. In the middle column, write how you think they might be put in plain language so that their meaning is clear. In the third column write briefly why you think the author has used these similes – for example, do they help you to understand a situation or feeling more vividly?

Chapter 19

One of the graves had a bunch of fresh wild flowers on it, and they started blowing about in the wind, and in the end they rolled right off the mound of grass and on to someone else's grave. I picked them up on my way out of the churchyard and bent down to put them back where they belonged. Something caught my eye, then. You know the way your own name leaps out at you. There was mine, green with moss, on the gravestone. Samuel. I knelt down to try to read the other letters, holding my broken glasses on with one hand.

MARGARET FRITH
Beloved wife of Samuel

Died in childbirth, 1980

I stood up so suddenly that I went giddy. That was the year I was born. I couldn't read the other letters. I didn't want to. Ellie Champion was wrong. My mother hadn't been a girl trudging over a mountain in a snow-storm. She had died giving birth to me. Here she was, buried in the churchyard, and her husband had named me after himself before he had given me away.

I spent that night in a barn. I couldn't afford to go on the camp-site and I knew there was no point putting up my tent anywhere or that farmer woman would be after me with her dog again. And at least the barn was dry. There were hens in it, though. I wasn't too happy about them because I thought they might bite me, so I kept myself well down in my sleeping bag. They clucked round me for a bit and then they hopped up onto posts and rafters and puffed themselves up for the night. Even through my sleeping bag the straw was really scratchy.

In the middle of the night an owl shrieked. It frightened the wits out of me. I thought it was inside the barn. I thought it might go for my eyes if I opened them. I didn't sleep a wink after that, not for hours. I'd meant to get away before dawn but I was woken up by the sound of the door being pushed open. Sunlight came rushing in like a flood of water, blinding me. I sat up with my hand shielding my eyes. A woman was standing in the doorway, staring at me.

Next day the house was so quiet. Like the end of the world with quiet.

Mam was on her bed under a sheet. Father was worn out with sorrowing. The boys were with Caroline at Uncle Staff's.

I went down to the field where the wild people's camp had been. Couldn't help it.

Wanted to see the horses still there, and the vans still parked. Wanted to hear the wild people laughing and talking.

Wanted to see Mam walking down to the lane with her arms folded over her big belly.

I would never see Mam again.

The field was torn up where the horses and tyres had trundled. Black rings where the fires had been. Nothing more.

I looked up and I saw the mist on the side of the mountains. All round me, rolling like water.

And I would never see him again, Sam, the wild boy.

Chapter 20

I don't think about the wild boy.

I don't think about his baby.

Try not to.

Tried not to the day Caroline found me in the snow. Kept it all out of my head. Kept my mouth shut. Kept my mouth shut for months.

Nearly died, Caroline told me, after I'd been over the mountain.

She nursed me. She fed me with bread dipped in milk, like Mam would have done.

She hung my black coat on the door-nail in my room. When I woke up I thought it was Mam. Wanted Mam.

I didn't talk. I got on with my jobs. I had to go into the barn every day, collecting the eggs with Michael. Always stopped, just there, by the doorway, waiting to see if the straw breathed in that corner. Always frighted, remembering that night.

'Shush-shush,' to the hens. 'Come shush-cluck.' Picked up the eggs and got out as quick as I could, every day.

When spring came the broody hen hatched out her eggs. Michael and I brought her thirteen chickens into the house. We put them in the chick basket by the fire. I knelt on the hearthrug with Peter and Michael to watch them. Caroline brought a saucer of water and set out the chicks to drink. One was too tiny, it lay on its side and didn't move.

I picked it up, saw it was breathing. Held its beak open so it could sip.

Caroline took the chick out of my hand, put it back in the basket, wiped my face with the kettle-rag.

'There, there, Elizabeth,' she said. 'You cry now. You cry.'

Chapter 21

I never wanted to be wed to anyone.

All those years after the wild people left, I never wanted to be wed. Nobody asked me.

Then one day Father came to me in the yard. 'Elizabeth,' he said. 'Joseph Rowlin has a mind to ask you to marry him, and I think you should say yes.'

I said nothing. Joseph Rowlin!

I walked away from my father, up to the pack-horse bridge. Stood there and looked over the whole valley, the whole long length of it, the dips and hollows, the walls and the fields, the sheep and the quiet cows. My lovely mountains and hills. Light on the grass was golden. Curlew bubbling like water. Skylark high, high up and singing his heart out. I've heard them every summer of my life.

Could see Father and Joseph together mending the walls. Michael and Peter are big boys now, I thought. Tall as me, don't need mothering. Mam is six years in the ground.

Caroline married and running the shop in the village. Uncle Staff dead. Could do with a man to help us with Uncle Staff's farm. I know that.

That skylark was bursting my ears with his singing. Be nice to have kisses again, Elizabeth Frith.

Joseph Rowlin was so timid, he didn't even look at me when I came back down to the yard. I went right up to him and he tried to pretend he didn't know I was there. 'Course he knew.

Could tell by his shoulders gone straight, the red on his neck. Could tell how frighted he was.

Skylark like splinters of crystal.

Held out my hand and touched Joseph's.

'Yes,' I said.

I put them out of my mind, the wild boy Sam, the baby in the straw. I put them out of my mind for ever.

Notes for Chapter 22

James spends the night in a barn and is awakened by a woman collecting eggs. Later, in the churchyard, he realises that he has jumped to the wrong conclusion. He decides to return home, but encounters some children playing in the river and teaches one of them to dive. Their mother comes to find them. James realises his quest is over.

What do you think?
This is the climax of the story. Consider Elizabeth's story so far and think about:
- why Elizabeth does not speak to James when she sees him
- what Meggie's natural ability to dive tells us.

Questions
Look for evidence to help you answer these questions:
1. How does James see the valley differently after meeting the woman in the barn?
2. Why is James' second visit to the village shop important to the development of the story?
3. How do James' two main interests in life come together in this chapter?
4. When do we realise James has found his birth mother?
5. Why doesn't James speak to Elizabeth? What does the last paragraph tell us about his feelings?

Further activity
James' father explained earlier why they chose not to call him Sammy. Berlie Doherty uses several first names more than once to show how people are related. In the real world, some families have names which appear frequently. Ask your friends and relatives if they have names which have been used by their families for generations. You may be able to find a book which gives the origin of a name (the language it comes from) and its original meaning. Make a list of the names in this book and of others which you have found from your research. Make a table with columns for each name, its origin, its meaning and how often it occurred in your researches. Use a word-processor to sort your list into alphabetical order and make frequency tables of the popularity of the names.

Chapter 22

The woman in the doorway of the barn must have seen me but she said nothing. She just stood there with her hand to her mouth, staring at me. I stayed absolutely still, hoping that she wouldn't start screaming or shouting at me or anything. She stared at me as if I was a spirit rising out of the straw.

Then she made this odd sound at the back of her throat, 'Shush-shush, come shush-cluck,' – an odd crooning, comfortable sound, a bit like the noise the hens made, and then she bent down and started fumbling round in the straw. I realised she was collecting eggs.

Her movements hypnotised me. She was probably about thirty but she looked a lot younger at first. She was very small and thin with light, untidy hair, and she bent and stooped like a dancer, balancing the basket across her arm and her hip. She concentrated totally on collecting those eggs, and all the time she was making that soothing clucketty sound at the back of her throat.

She never looked at me again, after that first moment. It was as if she had decided that I wasn't there at all. And I stayed so still that she might well have believed herself.

After she'd gone I waited a bit and then I gathered up my stuff and scurried out, sneaked round the back of the barn and ran off down the lane like a scared cat.

I stopped again after about half a mile. There was no one about. The sun was up full and streaming and every blade of grass was glittering with dew. I could hardly believe I was in the same place. It was like a different country when the sun shone. The slopes all glowed with purples and greens and yellows. There were little flowers on the lane-side, and blue and orange butterflies bobbing around them. I'd never been anywhere so pretty. I'd never heard so many birds singing – I don't know how so much noise could have come from such tiny creatures.

I walked down to the village shop and bought a can of juice with the last of my money. The woman there recognised me from the day before and chatted away to me about the weather and asked me if I'd be around for the Barn dance at the village hall on Saturday.

'My brother Michael is the fiddle player in the band,' she said. 'You ought to hear him.'

'I'll be in London on Saturday,' I told her.

'London!' she frowned. 'Pity you, I do. Who'd be in London when they could be here!'

I was just about to pluck up the courage to ask her if she knew where Samuel Frith lived when a voice called to her from the back of the shop.

'Caroline. Elizabeth's bringing the eggs. How many d'you want today?'

She excused herself and went away. I waited for a bit. I liked chatting to her. I went outside and sat on a wall near the shop to finish my drink and to eat some more of my dwindling supplies. Hardly any left, but it didn't matter. I'd be at Clair's by lunchtime. I couldn't decide whether I should try to find Samuel Frith or not. I didn't even know if I wanted to. The only thing I'd wanted was to see my mother, after all, just to see her. And I was fifteen years too late for that.

And yet, I still didn't want to go. Something was uttering in my head again. Something didn't make sense.

I wandered down the lane with my can in my hand and went back to the little graveyard. In the sunshine it wasn't a scary place after all. I wouldn't mind being buried there myself one day. When I'm dead, of course. I chuckled to myself as I thought that. It was the sort of thing Dad would have said. There were long-tailed birds, a bit like swallows, twitching across it, just touching the church wall and then skimming away again. They reminded me of little kids in the playground playing tick.

I went back to the gravestone and sat by it. Margaret, beloved wife of Samuel Frith, died in childbirth, 1980. Mother of … the names were so moss-ridden that I couldn't read them. I tried to think clearly. If Samuel Frith was my father, and he had all these other children, why did he need to have me adopted? Maybe he couldn't look after a very new baby himself. I supposed that would make sense. But why would he drive all the way round the valleys and arrive at Ellie Champion's door and plonk me in a letter-box, of all things? Why didn't he just ring up an adoption society and ask them to take me away?

Nothing really made sense at all. I traced the names, rubbing the moss off with the broken arm of my glasses. Beloved mother of Elizabeth, Caroline, Michael, Peter. And there was more writing. I had to pull the grass away with my fist to get to that. I scraped it clean.

'Also buried here, her child, who never lived to see the light of day.'

So I had been wrong. I leaned back, feeling total exhaustion. This gravestone had nothing to do with me, after all. I was back where I started.

I carefully replaced the grasses I'd pulled back, and the little bunch of wild flowers. I even wondered about trying to replace the lumps of moss I'd scraped out, squeezing them back into the engraved words. I felt as if I'd violated a private family grave. I went out of the churchyard and clicked the gate shut. I went back to the lane and turned towards the track that would lead me up to Horsenose Tor and away from the valley for ever.

I had looked at every house there. One of them must have been the one where I spent the first few hours of my life. I remembered what Ellie Champion said: 'She must have loved you, that child.'

I decided that I wouldn't stop again until I reached the narrow bridge over the pool where I'd tried to pitch my tent that first night. It seemed ages ago. Years ago. In a strange way I felt as if I'd become another person since then. Maybe it was something to do with being on my own, just talking to the quiet part of me inside my head for hours on end. I quite liked being with myself, I decided. I quite liked myself. I'd never thought of that before.

As I left the last of the farms and cottages behind I could hear the sound of children's voices squealing with laughter. They were playing in the river. I climbed on up towards them. There were about half a dozen children there, village children, I guessed, as there were no adults with them. It was one of the hottest days I could remember. I was gluey with sweat. I hadn't had a wash since I left the camp-site. I had definitely been living in my feet too long. I took my stinking trainers off and sat on the bank, dangling my feet in the icy water and wondering about stripping down to my under-pants and jumping in. The children were having a great time, splashing each other and shrieking their heads off.

I climbed up and sat by them, just watching. The pool under the bridge was so deep that you could easily swim in it, a few strokes across and back. The kids were jumping in from the bank and doggy-paddling across. I felt a desperate longing then to be in the water with them. I had pushed all that out of my mind and now it was hauling me back towards myself. I wanted to be in a long blue pool, stretching out my limbs to their full length, head down and ploughing through the water. I wanted to feel the silkiness of water against my skin, wanted to twist and spin in it and spiral down to the very deepest level. 'Touch base!' I could hear Ken Eldred saying. 'Touch base and stretch back up for home!'

One of the children, a yellow-haired girl of about eight or nine, climbed right up on to the side of the bridge and stood on it. The other children stopped playing and watched her. A little boy who looked as if he might be her brother scrambled up next to her, held his nose and

161

jumped in like a frog, arms and legs all over the place. But the little girl just waited, calm, for the water to settle again. She poised herself, slowly swung up her arms, and sprang, clean as an arrow, into the water. Her entry was perfect. I watched her dive again and again. She was a natural diver. It made my heart bump against my ribs to watch her. It made me think of something else Ken used to say. 'Some people are born to dive. I see kids diving every day of my life, and they're all good, but every now and again I see one who dives like a bird. It tightens my spine to watch them.' That's how he had felt, he said, the first time he'd seen me dive.

I went and stood on the bridge and waited for the girl to run up again. I had an urge to show her how to do a somersault.

'Hi,' I said to her.

She glanced at me and climbed on to the bridge side again. Her froggy little brother clambered up next to her.

'You're a pretty good diver,' I said to the girl.

'What's a diver?' the boy asked.

'Someone who jumps into the water like your sister does,' I said.

'Pooh,' he said, and fell off deliberately, making as much of a splash as he could.

'I do a lot of diving,' I said. 'I go to a special club where we're taught how to do it. You could join one, when you're older.'

She stared at me, her eyes round and solemn. I couldn't even tell whether she was listening to me or not.

'Shall I show you how to do a special dive?'

She still stared at me, registering nothing.

I crouched down and demonstrated, without jumping off myself, how she could do a forward somersault. She watched me in her calm way and then without a second thought she did it, letting me flip up her heels at the last minute so she could roll in. She didn't show a flicker of nerves.

'You could do it on your own now,' I told her. I went and sat down by the bank just so I could watch her doing it again. It was a special thing, to see her there with her skin gleaming in the sunlight and the greeny-purple mountains behind her, and the kids' laughter and shouting bouncing off the rocks. It all seemed much more natural than standing on a concrete slab and jumping into a big bath full of chlorine.

The other children left us after a bit, running off home for their lunches. The girl and her brother came and flopped down beside me. She lay on her stomach with her chin propped on her hands, staring up at me.

'You're very good,' I said.

She giggled then, covering her eyes up with her hands and squirming round on to her back.

'What's your name?' she asked me.

'Sammy,' I said.

'I'm Sammy,' her brother said. 'Aren't I, Meggie? I'm called Sammy.'

There it was again. A nagging, like an unfinished tune, was beating round in my head. There was a woman coming up the track towards us, very slowly. I didn't want to look up at her. I knew she had stopped and I knew she was standing with her hand just resting against her mouth. Now the beating inside me was so strong that it must burst out of me.

I realised that from somewhere out in the space beyond, the little boy, the little Sammy, was talking to me. 'What's in there?' he asked me. 'What's in your blue bag?'

'My swimming things,' I said mechanically. I unzipped my sportsbag. My hands were trembling. I still couldn't bring myself to look at the woman properly. 'My tent.'

'Mummy, he's called Sammy, too,' little Sammy said. 'And he taught Meggie to do a roly-poly off the bridge.'

'Your toothbrush. Your sleeping bag.' Meggie was giggling, rummaging through my bag. 'Haven't you got your jim-jams?'

'What's this?'

My ammonite had rolled out of the bag and Sammy picked it up. The woman let out a soft ah! of breath. You could hardly have heard it, it was so slight.

I knew what to do, then. The song was louder in my head than anything, louder than the noise of the river falling into the pool and away from it, or Sammy's prattling, or the voices of the sheep, louder than the unending chant of that bird. I took my ammonite from Sammy and went across to her with it.

She looked at me in the same way as she had looked at me in the barn that morning, as if she was seeing a spirit rising out of the earth, as if she daren't breathe in case she frightened it away. She took the ammonite out of my hand without a word and held it against her cheek.

'My snake-stone,' she said at last.

The children clamoured round her. 'What is it? What's a snake-stone? Why's he got it? Can I have it?' They were like the midges the other night, stopping me from thinking properly. I wanted them to go away and leave me with her.

There was someone else coming up the track towards us, a tall, yellow-haired man. Seeing me there he stopped and hung back, as if he was shy to talk to strangers. Or maybe he knew he was intruding.

'Elizabeth? Shall we eat now?' he called. The woman flinched a little, as if she was pulling herself out of a dream. She looked at me quickly, and in her look I saw a girl, scared. I saw her asking me something, and in my look to her I gave her my promise.

Both the children ran screeching down towards him. 'Daddy, Daddy, come and watch us dive.'

'After dinner,' he said. He hoisted Sammy on to his shoulders and stood with his hand on Meggie's head, waiting.

She handed back the snake-stone. 'Are you a happy boy, Sammy?' she asked me.

I nodded.

'I'm glad you're happy.'

I nodded again. There wasn't a word in me. She didn't have any more words in her, either. What use are words?

She stared at me as if she was trying to fix me in her

mind for ever. It was more than I could bear. I went to put my ammonite back in my sportsbag and when I stood up again she had gone away.

I watched her with her husband and her children, going slowly down the track to their home. I didn't go after her. I didn't want to. She had her own family. And so had I.

I didn't let myself look back again until I'd climbed to the very top of the Tor. A mist had come down, with the sun golden over it. The secret valley was hidden inside it.

Notes for Chapter 23

Elizabeth's story ends. We see that she is happy with her husband and her life. The events of long ago seem like a dream.

What do you think?
This is a very short chapter and is given over entirely to Elizabeth. The author has told her story in short bursts. Think as you read:
- how Elizabeth's story has been told throughout the book
- why her story ends here
- whether there are aspects of her life you would still like to know about.

Questions
It will help you to answer these questions if you take some time to look back through the sections of the book which tell Elizabeth's story.
1. How does the author change the time scale of Elizabeth's story to mirror what is happening in James' story?
2. How does the language used by Elizabeth change as her story progresses?
3. Why do you think that Elizabeth makes no attempt to talk further to James?
4. Do you think that by the end of her story that Elizabeth is happy?
5. What do you feel about what Elizabeth did with her baby?

Further activity
Much of Elizabeth's story uses imaginative or figurative language. This is often called imagery. For example, in this chapter she talks of words flying. Look at some of the other sections which tell her story and see how many times she uses such figurative language, either in single words or in short phrases. Collect these words and phrases into two lists, one of unpleasant images and the other of pleasant images. Why do you think the author uses such imaginative language in telling Elizabeth's story? What does it tell us about Elizabeth? How does it help you to understand her feelings more clearly?

Chapter 23

Joseph said to me, 'Elizabeth. What's the matter?'

I shook my head. Couldn't tell him.

He put his hands on my shoulders, lowered his face down to mine, the way he does. Little worry lights in his eyes. Little caring frowns.

'Elizabeth. Tell me.'

Shook my head again. Kept my hand to my mouth, lest the words flew out and hurt him.

Joseph laughed a little. 'Look like you've seen a ghost, love!'

A ghost. Was that what it was?

The ghost of the black-haired wild boy.

Notes for Chapter 24

James returns to a welcome at Horsenose Cottage. He writes to his parents to explain where he has been.

What do you think?
In this chapter we see how James' feelings for his birth mother and for his adoptive parents change. As you read, think about:
- how Clair's mother realises that James is not ready to talk about his experiences immediately
- why Ellie Champion decides she is getting better
- what James does to show that he has completed his quest.

Questions
1. Why does James feel he is coming home when he returns to Horsenose Cottage?
2. What does Ellie Champion say to James that shows she understands the decision he has come to about his family?
3. Why does James feel he needs to make Elizabeth real?
4. What does the letter James writes home tell you about how he feels about both of his parents?

Further activity
Write a description of Joseph Rowlin, his wife and family. You should start by giving as many details of their appearance as possible. Next, look for evidence in the text of their characters, behaviour, interests and any ambitions they might have. Try to write your description in the way that Berlie Doherty writes as Elizabeth, so that your work could form an extra chapter, at the end of the book or between Chapters 24 and 25.

Chapter 24

When I got back to Clair's I felt as if I was coming home. All through the long trek back I'd been going over and over in my head that strange meeting with my mother. I hadn't expected her to be married, or to have children. I suppose in a way, in a selfish sort of way, I'd expected her to have been waiting for me to turn up, and that she would have been really pleased to see me. I'd expected her to want to ask me all kinds of questions to fill in those years. I hadn't told her anything. I hadn't even told her about my diving.

I didn't know what to think any more. But I'd done what I'd set out to do. I'd found her. I'd actually seen her. I knew exactly what my mother looked like.

And something else had happened as well. I'd stopped thinking of her as my real mother. Mum was my real mother. I couldn't wait to see her again.

I was still working all this out when I arrived. Clair came running up the path to meet me.

'I saw you coming from the window,' she said. 'You've been ages! Did you find her?'

I nodded.

'Brilliant! Mum – he found her! What's she like? Was she pleased to see you?'

Her mother took one look at my face and said, 'I don't think Sammy wants to talk about it yet, Clair. I should think he's far more interested in having a bath, aren't you? And a hot meal?'

I was more tired than I'd ever been in my life. I sagged into the bath and just lay there for about half an hour, till Clair shouted up that a meal was ready for me. Her mother chatted to me about everything under the sun except my journey over the Tor, while Clair tutted and sighed and couldn't get a word in edgeways. After I'd eaten, and I was feeling bright enough to talk again, we took our cups of cocoa upstairs and sat with Ellie Champion.

'A lot has happened since you went away, young man,' she told me. 'Frances has decided that she's missing her husband and Tommy so much that they're going back home to London tomorrow.'

'I think we're planning to take Sammy with us. We'll make sure he gets to his coaching that way,' Clair's mother smiled at me.

'And I've decided I'm getting better,' Ellie said. 'I think it was meeting you again that did it, and seeing you striding away up the Tor there. And Frances threatened to take me back to London with her if I didn't perk up. Oh no! I'm not living in a city, not for anything. I think we all know where we belong, don't we, Sammy?'

She wasn't talking to me as if I was just a boy who'd wandered in from the street. She was talking to me like one grown-up talking to another.

'Actually, my name isn't Sammy,' I said. 'They call me James now.'

It made us all laugh, that. Funny how good that felt.

'Are you going to tell us about your mother?' Ellie asked.

I closed my eyes. 'She's very small,' I said. It was hard to picture her already. 'And thin. Tiny. She's got brown, shortish hair and her skin is very brown too. She's got a nice face. A lovely face, sad and lovely.'

There. I'd done it. I'd made her real. I opened my eyes again. Ellie was nodding at me, pleased with the picture I'd given her.

'Anything you'd like, before you go to bed?' Clair's mother asked me.

'Yes, please,' I said. 'Some writing paper. I think I'd like to write a letter to Mum and Dad.'

It took me ages to write a few words down. When I'd finished it I took it to the post office. It seemed years since I had stood there and first noticed Clair's mother in her blue dress. I'd felt like a little lost child then.

With a strange, disconnected feeling I let go of the letter and watched it slide through the slit. It would be at home when they arrived back from Scotland. I pictured Mum and Dad's face when they read it. I saw Mum putting on her reading glasses and peering at it, biting her lip, wondering. I saw Dad, his wide, smiling face, his surprised laugh. I was longing to be with them again.

I recited the words of the letter as I walked back to Horsenose Cottage. I knew them off by heart, it had taken me so long to get them right. What I wanted to say was that I wanted to adopt them. That was the sort of thing

Dad loved. He would have seen the joke of it. But it would probably have made Mum cry, and I didn't want that, so instead I wrote,

Dear Mum and Dad,

I haven't been where you thought I was going. I found the place where I was born, and I saw my mother, and I think I understand now why she gave me away. I know I can't stay with her. I just wanted to see her, that was all. I'm glad I did. And I'm glad I'm coming home.

Love,

James.

Notes for Chapter 25

James returns home. He takes part in the National Diving competition. He feels content with his life, and is enjoying diving again, now that his search is over.

What do you think?
The last chapter of a book is an opportunity for the author to tie up any loose ends. Elizabeth's part in the story has been told, but there are other questions which need to be answered. Think as you read:
- how James' mother has hidden her fears that he might leave
- how James now feels about his diving.

Questions
1. Why do you think James' dad leaves the room after hearing his story?
2. What does the author want us to feel about James' mum?
3. Why do you think James' diving has improved?
4. Do you think it is important for us to know if James is going to win the competition?
5. What does the author mean by the last sentence 'I was home.'?

Further activity
Look at the short descriptions on the covers or fly leaves of a range of books in a library or bookshop. You will see that these 'blurbs' as they are often called give enough information about the books to encourage people to read them, but do not give away too much in case they spoil your enjoyment of the story. Write a suitable 'blurb' for *The Snake-stone* which will encourage people of your age to try the book.

Chapter 25

On the day of the Nationals I was calm in a throng of jittery, nervous divers. Whatever happened, it was all right. It didn't matter if I didn't win the title. Mum had told me that in the hotel room the night before.

And I told her and Dad the whole story of my visit to the secret valley, and they didn't interrupt me once. When I'd finished she looked at Dad and he just ruffled my hair in a typical Dad way and went out of the room.

Mum said, 'When we decided to adopt you, we were taking a step into the unknown. We knew nothing at all about you, except that you'd been abandoned. I was very nervous, James. I kept looking at you and thinking, what will he be like? How do we know he's right for us? What if we don't like him? It took me about two days to be sure that I wanted you, and I've never, never changed my mind since. But last week, before you went away, I thought I'd lost you. I didn't know where you were going, but I had to let you go, and hope against hope that you would choose to come back.'

And there they were down in the spectator's gallery, along with Matt and his dad, and Clair. I've never had such a big following. And it didn't matter whether I won or not. That was the great thing.

I was diving well, though. I knew it. I felt good about everything. 'James Logan.' My name was called for the last round and I climbed up to the top board. The upturned faces blurred to a smudge of pink. I was on my own again. And I was very calm. This morning Ken said to me that I've been diving like a dream since I came back.

'That break must have done you good, after all,' he told me, scratching his chin. 'You're not diving like a kid obeying instructions any more. You're diving like a young man who knows where he's going.'

I walked to the edge of the board for my final dive, which I wanted to be my showpiece. I was counting slowly in my head. I stood, poised and calm. I spread out my arms, every nerve concentrated on what was to come, frozen into my waiting position. There wasn't a sound to be heard. I saw a misty valley, and a little girl with yellow hair standing on a bridge. I let her drift away, away out of my mind. My head was clear.

Then I swung up and out, up through my arms, up out of my waiting stance, till only air was holding me. I spun and spun again, another half spin. I was a curled-up snake falling like a stone out of the sky. And then I reached out and down, full stretch, long and taut and swift, and ripped clean through the water.

I was home.

Further reading

Other works by Berlie Doherty
Granny was a Buffer Girl (Heinemann, 1998)
Before she leaves home, Jess wants to find out all she can about her family's past. She finds out about her grandmother's life as a child worker buffing (polishing) cutlery for a big company. She finds what happened to her granny's hopes of a better life.

Spellhorn (HarperCollins, 1990)
Sam's friend, Laura, is blind, but claims to be able to 'see'. One night the mysterious 'Wild Ones' gallop into the village, burning the houses. Only Laura can see them. There follows a number of fantastic adventures in the world of the Wild Ones.

Some other books by Berlie Doherty:
Daughter of the Sea (Longman, 1999)
How Green You Are! (Egmont, 1992)
The Making of Fingers Finnigan (Egmont, 1993)
Tilly Mint Tales (Egmont, 1994)
White Peak Farm (Mammoth, 1994)
Children Of Winter (Mammoth, 1995)

Works with similar themes by other authors
A Serpent's Tooth by Robert Swindells (Puffin, 1995)
Lucy's parents are splitting up and she hates her new school. Hearing of plans to open a nuclear waste site, her mother moves with her to a women's protest camp nearby. Lucy discovers she has a remarkable gift which enables her to sense the terrible secret of Pit's Field.

Carrie's War by Nina Bawden (Puffin, 1993)
After her husband's death, Carrie takes her children on holiday to

the village in Wales where she spent the war. Searching for her past, she recalls the harsh treatment she and her brother suffered as evacuees, and the mysterious friends she made in an isolated house on the mountainside. Was it her fault that they have all moved away?

Jane Eyre by Charlotte Brontë (Puffin, 1994)
Set in the wild moorland of Yorkshire, this is the classic story of the orphan, Jane Eyre, who longs to be able to leave her unhappy life with her aunt's family. Her wish is soon granted, but not in the way she might have expected. We follow Jane's fortunes through many years of hardship until at long last she achieves happiness.

Programme of Study

Word

1. The following passages are taken from *The Snake-stone*. Some words have been left out. Without looking in the book to find what the author wrote, choose suitable words to fill the spaces, using your understanding of how Doherty uses language. Make sure that your chosen words make grammatical sense by reading each sentence to yourself with your chosen word in place.

Passage A

The tent was twice as bulky as it had been before and wouldn't go back into its bag, however much I _____ it and squeezed it. I'd wanted to _____ away before the farmer woman came round for the money but I was too late. She came _____ across the field in her wellies and with the dog joyfully _____ itself at crows behind her. She spoke to him once and he _____ over to her and crouched behind her. It must be _____ to have that kind of power.

Passage B

I walked away from my _____, up to the pack-horse bridge. Stood there and looked over the whole _____, the whole long length of it, the dips and hollows, the walls and the fields, the sheep and the _____ cows. My _____ mountains and hills. Light on the grass was _____ . Curlew _____ like water. Skylark high, _____ up and singing his _____ out. I've heard them every summer of my _____ .

2. Compare the words you have used with those used by a partner. Whose choices are better? Why do you think this is so?

3. Find the passages in the original text (Passage A is on page 139 and Passage B on page 154) and compare your words with those used by Berlie Doherty. Think about why you may have used the same words in some places, and what the effects are where the words are different.

Sentence

Berlie Doherty often writes Elizabeth's words in short, jerky sentences. This gives the impression that she is talking to us, or that she is worried and upset.

1. Read again the passage on pages 23–4 of Chapter 2 where Elizabeth is talking: 'Shushed to the hens; "Shush-shush, come cluckety-cluck," like I always do. ... I didn't know what to do with a live one.'

2. Rewrite the passage as if it were being told by a narrator. You might start by rewriting the first sentence like this:

Elizabeth quietened the hens, saying 'Shush-shush, come cluckety-cluck,' as she always did.

3. Compare the original version of the passage with your version. Which is the more effective? Why do you think this?

Look again at pages 164–6 of Chapter 22.

4. Read the passage which describes James' feelings as he hands the ammonite to Elizabeth: 'I knew what to do, then. ... held it against her cheek.'

5. Now read the last four paragraphs of the chapter (on page 165–6): 'I nodded again. ... The secret valley was hidden inside it.'

6. What do you notice that is different between the way these two passages are written? You might start by considering the language used, the length of sentences and so on. Why do you think the author has chosen to vary her style like this? What effects is she trying to achieve?

Text

1. Read Chapter 6 again. There are several conversations, some between James and his fellow pupils and some between James and his teachers. As you read them, think about the kind of language used in each conversation. For example, you may notice different uses of words and different lengths of sentences. Make a note of these differences, making it clear who is talking to whom. What do these differences tell you about the speakers and the circumstances?

2. In Chapter 13, Clair's mother tells James (whom she calls Sammy) that he should try tracing his mother through official agencies. Using any suitable means available to you, find out how James might have gone about this search in a more conventional manner. Write a set of instructions for him, based on what you find out about making such searches.

3. In Chapter 12, James comes to the village of Hollygate. He asks a group of women for directions. Read the chapter again. How would you present this chapter as a scene from a play or television script? Prepare a classroom drama script giving plenty of character and stage directions. Think carefully about how much information you need to include for actors who may not have read the book. Be careful also not to put in too much unnecessary detail which might confuse an audience.

4. *The Snake-stone* is a novel. This means that it is a work of fiction and is not a true story, although in the author's introduction we are told where many of the ideas for the story came from. What are your feelings about how believable the story is as regards:

- The events portrayed – do they seem possible?
- The way the characters behave – does this seem natural?
- The outcome – do you feel that it all works out too well?

5. Choose some passages where you feel that the author has, in your opinion, been particularly successful in convincing you of the reality of the characters and events. Look for other passages where you feel there has been an element of unreality or fantasy. Can you explain why the author has written each passage in this way? Compare your selections with those made by a partner. Which type of writing do you each prefer?

Glossary

13	**lurching:** walking unsteadily; tipping to one side
16	**sleuth:** detective
16	**satin:** shiny silken material
17	**pummelling:** pounding
18	**matineé jacket:** short coat – day wear for a baby
18	**drooling:** slobbering like a baby
21	**coma:** very deep sleep; stupor
24	**foyer:** large entrance hall
24	**frustrated:** thwarted; prevented from achieving a goal
25	**concertina:** musical instrument with folded bellows
28	**groundwork coaching:** basic skills teaching
29	**cascade:** waterfall; a loose, wavy flow of fabric
32	**psychos:** people who behave as if insane (a slang word)
33	**yodelled:** Tyrolean singing where the voice alternates rapidly between high and low
34	**gallows:** wooden frame for hanging criminals
37	**husky:** throaty; hoarse
40	**tor:** rocky hill or mountain
40	**boggarts:** terrifying ghosts or goblins
44	**option:** choice
47	**cred.:** short for credibility – status among young people (a slang word)
52	**Triassic era:** the time when dinosaurs lived, in the first part of the Mesozoic era, it lasted 45 million years
52	**Mesozoic era:** a period of geological time which began 225 million years ago and lasted about 155 million years and includes the Triassic era
53	**petrified:** turned to stone
54	**OS:** Ordnance Survey, the Government map-making office
55	**lunged:** plunged forward
60	**jossing:** joking

61	**voluntaries:** dives chosen by the competitor
64	**balked:** checked or stopped suddenly
65	**fantasised:** made up imaginary situations
65	**muffed:** bungled
69	**grouse:** moorland game bird
70	**contour lines:** coloured lines on a map showing regular divisions of height; closer lines represent steeper slopes
70	**methodical:** deliberately orderly
74	**sauntering:** strolling casually
77	**warbling:** singing in a quavering way like a bird
87	**vagrant:** homeless wanderer
96	**jugular:** jugular vein, one of three large veins in the neck
101	**deflated:** let down suddenly, like a balloon
101	**pompous:** ridiculously self-important
104	**gagging:** choking; feeling of sickness
104	**whirligig:** a spinning toy; a merry-go-round
104	**register:** show understanding
108	**quest:** a search, often with a religious aim
124	**yearning:** intense longing
127	**uncanny:** weird and unexpected
129	**skittered:** skimmed
133	**avalanche:** an unstoppable rush, often of snow
143	**pact:** firm agreement or promise
153	**kettle-rag:** cloth for lifting a hot kettle from an open fire
155	**crystal:** clear quartz like ice; very clear glass
157	**hypnotised:** transfixed; unable to move
160	**violated:** disturbed or desecrated
177	**throng:** crowd
178	**taut:** stretched tight

Title list

NEW LONGMAN LITERATURE

Post-1914 Fiction

0 582 43446 7	I'm the King of the Castle	Susan Hill
0 582 02660 1	The Woman in Black	Susan Hill
0 582 25399 3	The Mist in the Mirror	Susan Hill
0 582 06016 8	Brave New World	Aldous Huxley
0 582 06017 6	The Cone-Gatherers	Robin Jenks
0 582 06021 4	The Fifth Child	Doris Lessing
0 582 08174 2	Picnic at Hanging Rock	Joan Lindsay
0 582 06557 7	Lamb	Bernard MacLaverty
0 582 08170 X	Lies of Silence	Brian Moore
0 582 43447 5	Animal Farm	George Orwell
0 582 06023 0	The Great Gatsby	F Scott-Fitzgerald
0 582 43448 3	Daz 4 Zoe	Robert Swindells
0 582 29247 6	A Slipping Down Life	Anne Tyler
0 582 09714 2	To the Lighthouse	Virginia Woolf

Post-1914 Short Stories

0 582 28730 8	Quartet of Stories
0 582 23369 0	The Human Element & Other Stories
0 582 43449 1	A Roald Dahl Selection
0 582 28931 9	Stories Old and New
0 582 03922 3	Stories from Asia
0 582 25393 4	Stories from Africa
0 582 28928 9	Mystery and Horror
0 582 28927 0	War Stories
0 582 02661 X	Ghost Stories
0 582 28929 7	Global Tales
0 582 29249 2	Ten D H Lawrence Short Stories

Post-1914 Poetry

0 582 29248 4	Voices of the Great War
0 582 35149 9	Poetry 1900 to 1975
0 582 25401 9	Poems 2

Post-1914 Plays

0 582 30242 0	Absent Friends	Alan Ayckbourn
0 582 06019 2	The Winslow Boy	Terrence Rattigan
0 582 22389 X	P'Tang, Yang, Kipperbang & other TV plays	Jack Rosenthal

0 582 43445 9	Educating Rita	Willy Russell
0 582 08173 4	Shirley Valentine	Willy Russell
0 582 25383 7	Ten Short Plays	
0 582 25394 2	Scenes from Plays	
0 582 06014 1	The Royal Hunt of the Sun	Peter Shaffer
0 582 09712 6	Equus	Peter Shaffer
0 582 06015 X	Pygmalion	Bernard Shaw
0 582 07786 9	Saint Joan	Bernard Shaw
0 582 25396 9	The Rivals/The School for Scandal	Richard Brinsley Sheridan

Post-1914 Stories from other Cultures

0 582 28730 8	Quartet of Stories	
0 582 06011 7	July's People	Nadine Gordimer
0 582 25398 5	Heat and Dust	Ruth Prawer Jhabvala
0 582 07787 7	Cry, the Beloved Country	Alan Paton
0 582 03922 3	Stories from Asia	
0 582 25393 4	Stories from Africa	
0 582 28929 7	Global Tales	

Post-1914 Non-Fiction

0 582 25391 8	Genres	
0 582 25384 5	Diaries and Letters	
0 582 28932 7	Introducing Media	
0 582 25386 1	Travel Writing	
0 582 08837 2	Autobiographies	
0 582 01736 X	The Diary of Anne Frank	

Pre-1914 Fiction

0 582 07720 6	Pride and Prejudice	Jane Austen
0 582 07719 2	Jane Eyre	Charlotte Brontë
0 582 07782 6	Wuthering Heights	Emily Brontë
0 582 07783 4	Great Expectations	Charles Dickens
0 582 28729 4	Oliver Twist	Charles Dickens
0 582 23664 9	A Christmas Carol	Charles Dickens
0 582 23662 2	Silas Marner	George Eliot
0 582 22586 8	The Mayor of Casterbridge	Thomas Hardy
0 582 07788 5	Far from the Madding Crowd	Thomas Hardy
0 582 30244 7	Ethan Frome	Edith Wharton

Pre-1914 Collections

0 582 25405 1	Wessex Tales	Thomas Hardy
0 582 28931 9	Stories Old and New	
0 582 28927 0	War Stories	
0 582 25388 8	Characters from Pre-20th Century Novels	

0 582 25384 5	Diaries and Letters	
0 582 25385 3	Highlights from 19th Century Novels	
0 582 25389 6	Landmarks	
0 582 25386 1	Travel Writing	
0 582 33807 7	19th Century Short Stories of Passion & Mystery	

Pre-1914 Poetry

| 0 582 22585 X | Poems from Other Centuries | |

Pre-1914 Plays

0 582 25397 7	She Stoops to Conquer	Oliver Goldsmith
0 582 24948 1	Three Plays	Henrik Ibsen
0 582 25409 4	Doctor Faustus	Christopher Marlowe
0 582 28930 0	Starting Shakespeare	
0 582 43444 0	The Devil's Disciple	Bernard Shaw
0 582 07785 0	Arms and the Man	Bernard Shaw
0 582 28731 6	The Duchess of Malfi	John Webster
0 582 07784 2	The Importance of being Earnest	Oscar Wilde

NEW CENTURY READERS

Post-1914 Contemporary Fiction

0 582 32847 0	Granny the Pag	Nina Bawden
0 582 29254 9	The Real Plato Jones	Nina Bawden
0 582 25395 0	A Question of Courage	Marjorie Darke
0 582 32845 4	Daughter of the Sea	Berlie Doherty
0 582 43455 6	The Snake Stone	Berlie Doherty
0 582 29262 X	My Family and other Natural Disasters	Josephine Feeney
0 582 31941 2	The Tulip Touch	Anne Fine
0 582 43452 1	Flour Babies	Anne Fine
0 582 29257 3	A Pack of Liars	Anne Fine
0 582 29258 1	The Book of the Banshee	Anne Fine
0 582 29261 1	Madame Doubtfire	Anne Fine
0 582 29251 4	Step by Wicked Step	Anne Fine
0 582 29260 3	Goggle Eyes	Anne Fine
0 582 29255 7	MapHead	Lesley Howarth
0 582 43453 X	A Northern Childhood	George Layton
0 582 32846 2	Lizzie's Leaving	Joan Lingard
0 582 31967 6	Night Fires	Joan Lingard
0 582 43456 4	Goodnight Mister Tom	Michelle Magorian
0 582 43451 3	Journey to Jo'burg	Beverley Naidoo
0 582 36419 1	Aquila	Andrew Norriss

0 582 29256 5	Along a Lonely Road	Catherine Sefton
0 582 31966 8	A Serpent's Tooth	Robert Swindells
0 582 31968 4	Follow a Shadow	Robert Swindells
0 582 31964 1	Urn Burial	Robert Westall

Post-1914 Poetry

| 0 582 25400 0 | Poems 1 | |
| 0 582 22587 6 | Poems in my Earphone | |

Post-1914 Plays

0 582 43450 5	Mirad, a Boy from Bosnia	Ad de Bont
0 582 09556 5	Bill's New Frock	Anne Fine
0 582 09555 7	Collision Course	Nigel Hinton
0 582 09554 9	Maid Marian and her Merry Men	Tony Robinson
0 582 10156 5	The Fwog Prince	Kaye Umansky

Pre-1914

| 0 582 42944 7 | Oliver Twist | Charles Dickens |
| 0 582 29253 0 | Twisters | |